Decorations from Nature

Decorations from Nature

Growing, Preserving & Arranging Naturals

Linda Lee Lindgren

Photographs by Peter Benson
Line drawings by Nannette Lindgren Lynch

CHILTON BOOK COMPANY • RADNOR, PENNSYLVANIA

To my husband, Roy,
for sharing my dreams and making them come true.

Copyright © 1986 by Linda Lee Lindgren
All Rights Reserved
Published in Radnor, Pennsylvania 19089 by Chilton Book Company

No part of this book may be reproduced, transmitted or stored
in any form or by any means, electronic or mechanical,
without prior written permission from the publisher

Designed by Jean Callan King/Metier Industrial, Inc.
Manufactured in the United States of America

Library of Congress Cataloging in Publication Data
Lindgren, Linda Lee.
Decorations from nature.
Includes index.
1. Nature craft.   2. Dried flower arrangement.
I. Title.
TT157.L46   1986   745.92   86-9713
ISBN 0-8019-7696-0 (pbk.)

1 2 3 4 5 6 7 8 9 0   5 4 3 2 1 0 9 8 7 6

Contents

Acknowledgments

A big thank you to Peter Benson for his beautiful photography and his ability to show my work to its best advantage.

To my daughter Nannette Lindgren Lynch for her continued support and beautiful drawings.

To Jennifer and Carolyn for pitching in and helping when things at home got behind.

To my husband, Roy, for sharing his garage and basement, even though I always leave a mess.

To all my friends in the Guilford Garden Club for their support, interest and the sharing of their knowledge for the last twelve years, and for supplying me with their beautiful flowers.

To Mary for helping me grow the luffas—an interesting project to watch.

To Audrey and Joan for their patience in answering my never ending question, "What is this?"

To Ellie for helping with the decorations on the Thomas Griswold House, Guilford, Connecticut, at Christmas and her beautiful designs in the book.

To Shirley for her beautiful table design in the Christmas room.

To Chere Brodsky for her potpourri basket design on the Christmas tree.

To the Guilford Keeping Society for allowing me to use the front door and interior of the Thomas Griswold House for photography.

To Mary Jean McLaughlin for the use of the front door at A Summer Place in Guilford, for the loan of her home and beautiful antique wicker furniture, and for her help during the many hours of photography.

To Page Hardware Store for the loan of their ladder and to Fonicello's Garden Center for supplying the natural green roping for the Thomas Griswold House.

To Mr. and Mrs. John English for the use of their home for photographing their beautiful porthole window.

To William Pinchbeck for supplying all the yellow roses for the Christmas designs.

To all the companies and manufacturers that supplied me with their products and beautiful dried materials.

And a special thank you to Kathryn Conover for her constant help and support.

Introduction

As a member of the Guilford Garden Club in Guilford, Connecticut, for the past twelve years, I have been actively growing, preserving and arranging fresh and dried flowers for my home and as a floral designer for various women's magazines. Each year the Garden Club presents a Harvest Bazaar, selling decorative items made from all natural materials that we have grown or collected from the roadsides. Ideas and information are shared among the members, always in search for something new to grow and preserve.

Each member has her own library of gardening and floral design books from which to gather information. The library collection is extensive, offering many sources of ideas and information. At our monthly meetings, experts in the various areas of floral design and horticulture add to our knowledge and abilities.

The information presented in this book is my attempt to consolidate as much information as possible under one title, offering you the opportunity to sample the many methods of plant drying and preserving, and giving you a few suggestions for the use of your newly found talents.

Nature presents us with her beauty throughout all the seasons of a year and is a never ending source of inspiration for beautiful designs if one will only look and see.

Flowers from the Garden

Drying and preserving flowers and foliage was an important part of gracious living during Colonial and Victorian times. Gardens produced an abundance of beautiful flowers, and the housewife was skilled in preserving and arranging flowers for her home, church and friends. A visit to Colonial Williamsburg is a walk back in time, and the elaborate period designs displayed are a testament to the housewife and her ability to use the flowers she grew.

Our gardens today may not support the wide variety or the volume of flowers grown in those days. But no matter how small the garden, there are many flowers to be dried or preserved for your continuous use and enjoyment. Seed and plant catalogs contain a wide variety of flowers suitable for drying, many which can be grown in containers or small gardens. Begin your selection by obtaining the catalogs and become familiar with the varieties and sizes of the flowers listed. The hardest part is to choose one over another. Dividing and sharing plants with friends is an excellent way of adding a new variety to your garden and keeping the size of the garden under control. Many perennials will spread and take over if not controlled. Dividing is also beneficial for many plants, promoting better blooming and healthier plants.

As your garden begins to grow and bloom, begin your drying and preseving. The earliest little spring bulbs can be preserved in silica gel for miniature arrangements in the house.

Weeds and Wild Plants

Wild roadside grasses and other spring plants and weeds are good sources of dried materials. "Weeds," as defined in the *Britannica World Language Dictionary*, are "any unsightly or troublesome plant that grows in abundance; especially, any coarse, herbaceous plant growing to injurious excess on cultivated or fallow ground where it is not wanted, as dock, ragweed, etc." Professor W.J. Beal, weed specialist at Michigan State University, lists a weed as a plant out of place. The *Oxford English Dictionary* defines a weed as a herbaceous plant not valued for use or beauty, growing wild and rank and regarded as cumbering the ground or hindering the growth of superior vegetation.

It is my hope and intent in this book to show you some of the reasons to value and use the many plants listed as weeds and "cultivate" those needed in abundance. Many volumes have been written about the origin of "weeds," those native to North America and those introduced from other countries. I have listed various sources in the bibliography for further reading.

Ralph Waldo Emerson, American poet, commented that a weed is "a plant whose virtues have not been discovered." The distinction between a wild flower and a weed may very well be the intended use or charm displayed by the plant in question. The Weed Society of America has studied weeds and listed the good and bad attributes of the various plants.

It is now known that weeds definitely have positive good traits: the deep roots of various weeds open up the soil for other shallow-rooted plants, bringing the deeply stored nutrients closer to the surface. Composting the weeds returns nutrients to the soil that would otherwise be lost to the shallow-rooted plants, as well as adding humus to the soil. Some weeds give off insect-repelling odors and act as beneficial companion plants.

However, there are bad side effects of some weeds, such as the buttercup. The roots of the buttercup secretes a poisonous substance and inhibits the growth of other plants nearby. If you cultivate buttercups for your dried flower pictures, it would be wise to choose an area where you are not trying to grow other more useful and desirable plants. The ever-abundant dandelion gives off ethylene gas that inhibits the growth of neighboring plants, yet the deep growing roots help to loosen and improve the quality of the soil, and dandelions produce a supply of early spring leaves for salads.

Collecting Wild Plants with Care

Begin your collecting of wild plants by becoming familiar with the plants in your area. Contact a local garden club or cooperative extension service for a list of the protected plants in your area. Plants and flowers on that list are in danger of becoming extinct and we all should be conservationists of our natural resources. Do not pick a flower or plant in any area if you see only one or two in bloom or growing. Very likely it is a rare or endangered plant.

Do not pick or collect any type of plant or flower along a state highway or in a state park. It is against the law and you may be arrested and fined. Choose areas along back roads and abandoned lots or fields to pick. Always secure permission from property owners when possible before picking any plant. Most people are willing to let you pick the wild grasses and weeds from their property, but ask first. Pick only small amounts from any one area, leaving flowers and seed heads for next year's growth. Never pick the last few flowers that are blooming in an area. You may completely deplete that plant from the area.

If you have children, they can also be enlisted in your efforts and given the pleasure of "helping" you pick the weeds and flowers; otherwise they may never ride in your car again after the first little green bug or spider alights on their head or arms. Take them with you and teach them the pleasures of seeing and experiencing nature at its finest. Teach them about plants, careful collecting, conservation of endangered species, and preserving of our wild areas. Give them an area in your garden to grow their own flowers, then teach them how to preserve the beauty they have grown.

The identification of the various poisonous and harmful plants is a very necessary part of collecting and using plants and weeds for any of your decorating efforts. When collecting plants for drying and decorating, knowing which plants cause skin irritation and rashes is most important. Knowledge of the poisonous parts of those decorative plants will help you protect your family, especially your small children. The color and appeal of berries to children is well known and many a child's death could have been prevented by a little knowledge and care.

Some of the most common plants with poisonous properties are:

Azaleas—foliage and flowers
Buttercups—leaves and flowers
English ivy—leaves
Foxglove—Leaves, seeds and flowers
Holly—berries
Iris—flowers and leaves
Poinsettia—leaves and sap of plant
Lantana camara—Foliage and fruit
Larkspur—all parts
Oleander—all parts, even dead and dried stems
Philodendron—all parts
Rhubarb—leaves

Swedish ivy—leaves
Wandering Jew—leaves
Yews—berries

Protect your children by teaching them to never eat berries or any parts of a plant unless it has been given to them by you or someone they know and trust.

Storage and Workspace

Carry home only the amount of materials you can handle and preserve in the time you have. Strip all leaves from the stems and hang the plants to dry as soon as possible after picking. The main idea is to remove moisture from the flowers as soon as possible to preserve the brightest colors.

Select a working and storage area for your dried plants and flowers. An attic or closet is often best because they are dark, dry and warm. Basements are generally damp during the summer months, and dampness is the worst enemy of dried plants. A garage is a good place to hang your bundles of "weeds." With a large piece of peg board nailed to one wall, small bunches of flowers can be wired to the hooks, keeping things organized and neat. Nails placed high on the rafters offer an out-of-the-way spot for large bundles until the plants are dry and ready to arrange.

Your primary work space for arranging will probably be the kitchen table at first, as the mess created by dried arranging is easily cleaned up. A special table set up on a porch or patio would be a good idea when you are making large arrangements or wreaths using materials that shatter heavily. I try to make as many of my wreaths as possible with the fresh, green materials and then hang the wreath to dry. Cutting and wiring the green stems to bases, or pushing the stems directly into straw bases, reduces the amount of shattering and half my work is finished. Working outside whenever possible also helps to keep the inevitable tag-along bugs outside too. Certain creatures of nature truly belong outside in their own habitat.

The plants and flowers used within this book are native to the

Northeast and many other areas of the country. However, if you are unable to find the particular flowers or plants I've used, try the preserving methods on the plants you have at hand. It is impossible to list every plant that dries and preserves successfully. But by picking, drying or preserving the plants native to your area, you can enjoy the beauty of nature throughout your home all year long.

PART ONE

Collecting and Preserving

Spring Dried Flowers

Acacia: Early spring blooming in semitropical areas. The most commonly known variety is mimosa; both flowers and foliage are used by florists extensively. The fluffy yellow flowers are fragrant and dry easily. Leave the grey-green foliage on the stems and hang branches to dry, or try leaving the branches in containers to dry. As they dry, interesting curved pieces will develop adding graceful lines to arrangements.

Achillea: A well-known wildflower with many cultivated garden varieties as well. All dry equally well by hanging. The most widely known common name is *yarrow*. The wild variety grows in late spring and has large, white umbels of flowers and grey-green, lacy foliage. Pick the flowers just as they are beginning to show color, before the individual flowers have opened. The white color will be more intense than if they are left to open completely. There are many side shoots on the stems, so only the flower head should be picked in order to provide continuous bloom and more flowers. Go back to the picking spot many

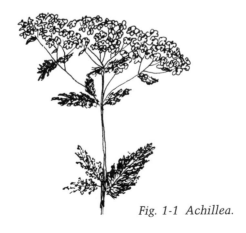

Fig. 1-1 Achillea.

9

times during the growing season for the successive bloom. Secure the flower stems to a coat hanger with rubberbands and hang to dry.

Ajuga: A popular rock-garden plant that blooms extensively from May to June with flowers ranging from white to pink and blue. All colors dry easily and retain their shape. Cut stems and secure to a coat hanger with a rubberband. Hang to dry. Stems will need to be attached to florist picks or other stems for support when used in wreaths or arrangements.

Allium: There are over 500 varieties of the onion family, each having an attractive flower head that dries easily. Most are cultivated for use in cooking, so their large ball-shaped flowers are a bonus to the dried flower arranger. Pick the flowers when they are fully opened and before seeds begin to form. They may be suspended in clusters on a coat hanger, but better results will be achieved if the stems are placed in a small amount of water and the flower allowed to dry upright in the container.

Cattails: A well-known dried accent material. Grows in inland wetlands or edges of streams and ponds. Pick as soon as the cattail develops and begins to turn brown. Spraying with hair-spray or plastic coating will help to seal the seeds and prevent shattering.

Clover: The wild purple clover is abundant in most areas. The deep purple flower heads are easily dried and make excellent accent material in spring wreaths. Pick individual flowers with short stems because more flowers will develop on the plant. Attach to a coat hanger with rubberbands and hang to dry, or wire to florist picks and add to a summer wreath while fresh. The colors will fade in time, but they are so abundant that a fresh amount can be picked each spring rather than saving the dried blooms from one season to the next.

Dandelion: Everyone knows the wild wanderings of a fluffy head of a dandelion, but if the seed head is picked at the right stage the seed heads will hold and can be used in arrangements. Pick the seed head when the white ends are just beginning to show and pick as long a stem as possible. Support the head by suspending it in a drying box, punching a hole and inserting the stem. Do not crowd the seed heads but leave space for the fluffy heads to open. The stems will dry stiff and the seed heads will not shatter easily.

Dock: A wild field flower common to most areas. Seed heads develop in later spring and may be dried in all stages of green through deep brown. Hang upside down or stand in a tall container and allow heads to develop graceful curves.

Fig. 1-2 Dandelion.

Grasses: There are over 4500 species of grasses with Latin names unfamiliar to most everyone, and yet the grasses are easily recognized in all areas. Pick the roadside grasses in early spring just as the heads develop and they will retain their soft green colors. Allow to develop further into the summer and fall and pick in the different color stages. Hang in bunches to dry; the heads will curve after drying when placed upright in containers.

Mullein: There are two useful parts to the mullein. One available in the spring is the soft, grey-green rosettes of leaves. Since the mullein is a bi-ennial, it takes two years for a flower stalk to develop. The seeds are dropped in early fall and begin to grow a small plant. In early spring the plant begins its growth and the tall seed head develops. The soft

Fig. 1-3 Dock.

11

Fig. 1-4 Wild grasses.

rosette can be picked either in late fall or early spring. Pick the small, tight center or the whole leaf cluster; each will dry easily. Cut the plant at ground level using a knife to cut through the heavy root. Do not pull the plant as the leaves will be damaged and bruised. The leaves tend to curl into the center if not supported and separated while drying. Place the plants in shallow boxes and separate the leaves with pieces of tissue paper, shaping leaves into curves to add interest to the flower shape. Large leaves may be dried individually and used in arrangements. Pick the tall seed heads in the fall and dry by standing in a container.

Muscari: Grape hyacinth is one of the earliest blooming spring

Fig. 1-5 Mullein—seed stalk and leaf rosette.

Fig. 1-6 Pussy willow.

bulbs, and the small seed pods that develop can be air dried easily. They are excellent in small Victorian arrangements in small containers. Pick while seed heads are green and stand in a container so that the seed heads have a natural appearance.

Mustards: Easily recognized yellow wildflowers with multiblooming stems. If left to develop, each variety produces interesting seed heads. Pick the flower stems when the flowers have just opened and hang to dry. Pick the seed heads while the seeds are still green and hang to dry. Flowers or seeds make excellent fillers in mass arrangements.

Pussy Willow: A wild or cultivated shrub producing small fuzzy catkins along slender branches in early spring. Pick pussy willows just as they have opened before the yellow pollen develops. Stand in tall containers until dry.

Summer Dried Flowers

Asclepias: Orange butterfly weed. A beautiful wildflower that received its name from the fact that it attracts butterflies all summer. This is a protected plant in many states and should not be picked. It is available from many seed catalogues and mail-order plant catalogues and is easy to grow in your own garden. The orange blossoms will dry by air method but are best preserved in silica. The seed pods that develop in the fall resemble a milkweed pod, yet much smaller. Pick after the seeds have been broadcast for new plants.

Achillea: "The Pearl" blooms profusely all summer. The small clusters of white flowers are picked with short stems and hung to dry on coat hangers. Dried flowers remain white after drying and are excellent filler material for wreaths. Stems may be attached to florist picks or longer dried stems for arrangements.

Agapanthus: "Lily-of-the-Nile" have large, exotic round flower heads in blue or white. Allow flowers to drop and save the dried seed head for large arrangements. Glue silver dollars (lunaria) among the stems and create a beautiful dried "flower."

Artemisia: Large number of varieties available, all equally useful for dried arrangements or wreaths. Allow to grow until early fall and pick the full length stem. Do not pull the plant as this is a perennial and will continue to grow and spread in the garden each year. Hang in bunches to dry.

Astilbe: A perennial easily grown in partial shade and damp soil. Colors range from white to pink and red. Pick the fluffy spires and hang to dry (they will shrink a great deal) or preserve in silica, which will retain the size of the flower. These are very attractive in mass arrangements as a color filler. Individual flower spikes press well and are useful in pressed flower pictures.

Baby's Breath: Popular, airy wisps of white or pink flowers filling large bracts. Easily dried by hanging. Pick when flowers are fully opened.

Fig. 1-7 Astilbe.

A second bloom may develop on the plants in early fall. Use as filler in arrangements and on wreaths.

Baptisia: "False indigo" has blue-grey foliage with lupin-like flowers that may be dried in silica. The seed pods are the most attractive and useful part of this plant for use in dried arrangements. The stems are very strong and the seed pods turn a deep, rich brown, almost black.

Catananche: "Cupid's Dart" is an easily grown annual with blue flowers and silvery bracts. Use either the flowers or the silvery bracts in arrangements. Hang to dry.

Celosia: Very popular summer annual blooming in shades of pink, peach, red and orange. Two types: plumed or cockscomb. Easily grown

Fig. 1-8 Celosia-plumed.

15

and self-seeds each year if flower bed is left undisturbed each fall. Transplant spring plants to thin. Cut flower heads at peak of color and hang to dry.

Chinese Lantern: Showy orange lantern-like calyces that dry easily on long stems. They are a perennial and multiply by sending runners under ground. Will tend to take over a garden. Pick in early fall when lanterns are bright orange. Hang to dry. Pretty, star-like flowers can be made if the lantern is cut open with scissors. The center has a large red berry that is an attractive center to the flower. Hold the petals open with tissue paper until petals have dried.

Cimicfuga: "Snakeroot" has tall plume-like branching flower spikes. Cut and hang the tall spikes for arrangements.

Clematis: Numerous types of vines with large flowers. Flowers may be pressed or dried in silica. If allowed to mature the flowers produce fluffy white heads that dry easily. Pick just as the heads begin to open and they will be more permanent. If left to dry on the plant they will shatter easily.

Delphinium: Annual and perennial varieties available in wide range of colors. May be air dried if picked when flowers are half open and half in bud on the long stems. May be dried in sand or silica for larger flowers and better color retention.

Echinops: "Globe thistle" is a hardy perennial that blooms profusely on long stems. Pick large globes when they have turned a deep grey-blue, but before the small flowers appear. If allowed to open fully,

Fig. 1-9 Chinese lanterns.

16

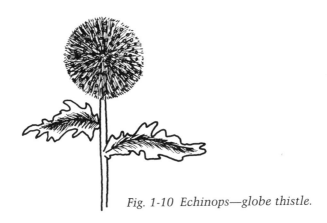

Fig. 1-10 Echinops—globe thistle.

the seed heads will shatter. Hang to dry in bunches. Remove the prickly leaves carefully with a knife or scissors.

Eucalyptus: A readily available commercial product that is grown in warmer climates. It has a pungent scented odor, with round leaves closely spaced on long stems. In its natural growing condition it is a soft gray-green color. It may be air dried or treated with a glycerine solution. Commercial products are treated and are available in a number of colors.

Everlastings: A name given to several species with flowers of papery quality. Included are lavender, globe amaranth, statice, cupid's dart and strawflowers. Strawflowers are grown from seeds each spring and are

Fig. 1-11 Everlastings.

17

available in a wide variety of colors and sizes. Pick the flowers when they are mature. The stems are very soft, so each individual flower will need to have a wire attached to the flower head after picking. Push the wire up through the center of the flower and back down, twisting the ends together at base of flower. Stand the flower in a vase or push the wire into a piece of Styrofoam until flower is dry. Color retention on these flowers is excellent and well worth the trouble to grow and preserve.

Feverfew: A tiny white, multi-flower of the crysanthemum family and the only one that will dry successfully. Pick the tiny button blooms, wire together and hang to dry. Excellent as filler material and in miniature arrangements.

Globe Amaranth: A paper-like flower that resembles a clover blossom in bright purple, pink, white, peach or orange. It is a tender annual and must be planted each season and the flowers harvested before frost. The stems are semi-soft and should be wired as with strawflowers (everlastings). One of the most colorful of the natural dried flowers; little or no fading of colors after drying.

Goldenrod: An abundant roadside perennial that is blamed for causing hayfever, when actually it is the ragweed that is to blame. Both are in bloom at the same time; ragweed is less showy, so not noticed. Goldenrod may be picked in various stages, the most successful for drying is just as the color begins to show on the green tips. Color will continue to develop after picking, so don't wait too long or they will shatter easily after drying. Bunch together and hang to dry. May also

Fig. 1-12 Globe amaranth.

Fig. 1-13 Goldenrod.

be preserved in glycerine solution and used indefinitely. Flowers turn a golden color; leaves and stems turn a warm brown.

Heather: All heaths and heathers are used by the florist for dried flower arrangements. Easy to grow in the garden. Flowers should be picked as they begin to open; bunch and hang to dry. The small needle-like foliage will drop after drying but the flowers will be semi-permanent. The stems are brittle when dry, so care must be taken when arranging. Cutting heather encourages growth and future blooms because blossoms are formed on new growth each spring.

Humulus: (Hops) Golden, papery heads on graceful vines. They are found growing along roadsides, covering trees and shrubs. Cut lengths of vine, removing the sharp hooks and leaves. This is a lot of work but worth the effort because the vines have beautiful tendrils that add interest to a wreath. May be added to a twig wreath or used to make a wreath of hop vines only.

Hydrangea: A large garden shrub with large clusters of showy white, green, blue, and pink flowers. All may be dried by hanging the large flower heads upside down. Pick them at different stages of growth and color change throughout the summer and early fall. The flower heads are very fragile when dry, but there is an abundance of flowers on one stem to work with. Use as a single flower in a large arrangement, or break off individual clusters of flowers for wreaths.

Iris: Large number of varieties available, from the large bearded to the small Siberian. Flowers of the bearded variety do not dry or preserve,

19

but the seed pods are large and attractive. All varieties produce seed pods in the fall. The small Siberian will dry and retain it's color, either in full flower or bud. Hang each individual flower until dry for use in a wreath or arrangement.

Jacaranda: A large tropical American tree with lacy foliage. The seed pods produced are round, flat disks and have an interesting center when opened before drying. They have a tough, thick skin, so care should be taken when cutting open. Use on wreaths, in corsages, or as focal points in an arrangement attaching to a long stem or florist wire.

Joe-Pye Weed: Large, full head of rose-pink flowers blooming on tall stems. Begins to bloom in late summer and must be picked in tight bud to retain the most color. If picked after the flowers have opened, the color is a muted pink and not nearly as pretty. Found along roadsides and in fields. Bunch together and hang to dry.

Kalanchoe: A perennial pot or greenhouse herb with large velvety leaves. Air-dry by laying on paper or hanging. Interesting curled shapes will develop.

Lavender: Old-fashioned herb used for potpourri. Pick as buds form to retain fragrance. Hang in bunches to dry. May be used in small arrangements to add some blue color. Leaves are also fragrant and can be used in potpourri.

Lichens: Found in damp areas of the woods and on old trees. Cut or break away. Dry in an oven at 250 F to kill spores. Wire into contrived flowers or glue to pinecones for interesting shapes.

Larkspur: Garden annual available in pinks, lavenders and white. Dries easily by hanging in bunches.

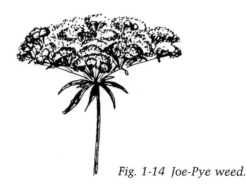

Fig. 1-14 Joe-Pye weed.

Liatris: Popular tall, spikey flowers ranging in colors of lavender and pink. Fluffy flowers open at the top of the spike and progress downward. Pick when spike is almost fully in bloom and hang to dry. White variety does not dry well.

Lily-of-the-Valley: Small graceful spike of white blossoms with heavy fragrance. Pick and dry in small arrangements, allowing the water to evaporate. Color turns a soft, light beige.

Locust Tree: Seed pods are glossy-brown and air dry easily. May be used on wreaths or wired to stems for arrangements.

Lotus: Pods are bowl-shaped and the top is dotted with round holes. They dry to a rich, dark brown and are used as focal points on a wreath or in an arrangement. Usually purchased from florists.

Luffa: Unusual cucumber-shaped plant material. When dry the interior is fibrous and rough. Grows on a heavy vine and requires a long growing season to mature. May be used whole or cut into cross-sections and flower shapes made from the pieces. May be purchased from a garden center or from the bath department in a large department store (used for removing dry skin during a bath or shower).

Lunaria: (Honesty or money plant) Tall plant producing purple flowers in the spring that develop into round, flat seed pods in later summer. As the pods mature the outer covering turns brown and can be removed easily, revealing silvery "dollar." The seeds will self-sow and start a new plant for next year's production as this is a biennial. Cut and hang to dry when seed pods are beginning to turn brown. Use in arrangements or add individual pods to pine cones or teasels for a contrived flower.

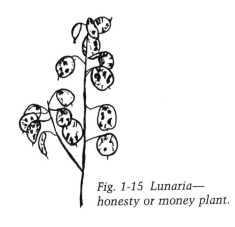

Fig. 1-15 Lunaria—
honesty or money plant.

Magnolia: A large evergreen tree or shrub. Leaves may be dried or treated in glycerine solutions and will remain pliable indefinitely. Flowers may be dried in silica but are very fragile. Seed pods are large and interesting for use in wreaths. Seal with plastic spray fixative.

Monarda: (Bee balm) A protected plant in the wild, but easily grown in a perennial garden. Large, shaggy heads with bright pink to red petals. Pick stem and hang to dry and some of the flower petals will remain. Large seed head is excellent as center for corn husk flowers or other contrived flower. This is a member of the mint family and has a pleasant aroma. The lavender pink variety was used to make Oswego Tea; it can also be dried for use in arrangements.

Nigella: (Love-in-a-mist) Old-fashioned garden annual that self-sows easily. Blue or white flowers surrounded by lacy foliage; seed pods are streaked with some color. Pick as pod begins to open and shed the seed. Leave some of the lacy leaves around the pods. Hang to dry.

Origanum: (Wild oregano) Relative of the herb oregano with some aroma in the leaves, but aroma disappears when dry. Purple buds develop and open into pink flowers in clusters. Pick clusters before the pink flowers open and the purple color will be retained. Strip the leaves and hang in small bunches to dry. Add to herb wreaths, attaching to a florist pick or use in small arrangements.

Osage Orange: Chartreuse inedible fruits with an unusual bumpy surface. Semi-permanent when left whole, but may be sliced and oven dried. Air drying is possible if cut thin. Add to dried wreaths or wire to stem for arrangements.

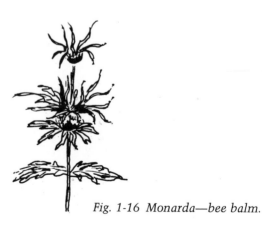

Fig. 1-16 Monarda—bee balm.

Fig. 2 *Fall wreath of dried dock, bleached grass heads, and orange star flowers. Photographed at The Thomas Griswold House, Guilford, CT.*

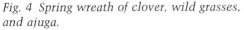

Fig. 4 *Spring wreath of clover, wild grasses, and ajuga.*

Fig. 3 *Oval grapevine wreath with seed pods and "flowers" of citrus peel.*

Fig. 5 *Corn husk wreath on Styrofoam base, decorated with corn husk flowers and celosia. Photographed at The Thomas Griswold House, Guilford, CT.*

Fig. 1 **Overleaf:** *Classic Colonial fruit fan and apple tree provide a Christmas welcome to family and friends. Photographed at The Thomas Griswold House, Guilford, CT.*

Fig. 6 **Opposite:** *A Colonial holiday setting: artemesia wreath with white lights, blue and white sideboard decor, and dining table centerpiece.*

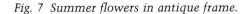

Fig. 7 *Summer flowers in antique frame.*

Fig. 8 *A massive autumn arrangement of gold yarrow and glycerine-treated sweet fern, goldenrod, eucalpytus, and rhododendron, flanked by a simple wreath of corn husk strips accented with corn husk flowers and foliage and a yellow and white fall floral candle ring, to which colored flowers can be added to accent changing table settings.*

Fig. 9 *Corn stalks, grasses, and dried flowers in an antique crock, designed by Jacqueline Plant and photographed at The Thomas Griswold House, Guilford, CT.*

Palms: All parts of a palm are useful in dried arrangements. Embryos of the date-palm open into interesting shapes. Soak the spathes in warm water to soften and shape or cut to any desired pattern. Weave strips into contrived flowers.

Pampas Grass: Exotic, tall-growing ornamental plant with fluffy plumes. Grows to a height of 6 to 8 feet with plumes 18 to 24 inches long. Available in white or pink from garden catalogues. Cut plumes and air dry.

Phragmites: (Reeds) Tall perennial grass that grows along the shore. Six to eight feet tall with fluffy plumes. Plumes begin to open in early summer and are a soft purple, but quickly turn to soft white or beige. If picked early enough, the purple color will remain. Picked at the end of the season the heads will be very full and fluffy. Cut and stand to dry. Use as filler in large arrangements. Spray with paint to change the colors.

Protea: Grown in Australia, South Africa or California, a large, unusual flower that dries beautifully. Looks somewhat like an artichoke, but has a soft pretty center when opened and in full bloom. May be purchased from florists or garden centers.

Queen-Anne's-Lace: Member of the parsley family that grows profusely along roadsides. Filmy white flowers on large rounded umbels. Umbels will curl upward and into a cup as they dry. Pick when flowers have just opened and dry by supporting in a drying box. Some may curl, but will still be useful in arrangements. Stems may be placed in colored water and flowers will absorb the color, then may be pressed for dried

Fig. 1-17 Queen-Anne's-lace.

23

flower pictures. Stems will absorb a glycerine mixture, turning the flowers a soft creamy color and the foliage a warm brown. Use in arrangements or wreaths. Dried umbels are picked in all stages and sprayed with paint or left natural to be added to dry arrangements.

Rudbeckia: (Black-eyed-Susan) Various varieties of this popular daisy-like flower with bright petals and dark centers grow in fields and along the roadsides. Flowers will dry well in silica and some varieties will air dry. Try both methods. The flowers wilt easily, so carry water in a container and place fresh-picked flowers in the water until you return home. The dark centers may be used for contrived flower centers.

Rushes: Large family of grass-like plants that grow in damp, marshy areas. Rushes have round, unjointed stems and grow to varying heights. All will air dry easily and retain their color and form. Use in mass arrangements.

Salvia: A large family of plants including annual, biennial and perennial varieties, ranging in color from deep purple-blue, blue and red. All may be air-dried. Pick when flowers have fully opened on the stem, but leave the side shoots to develop into more flowers. Remove leaves and hang in small bunches to dry. Excellent color material for arrangements and herb wreaths.

Sansevieria: (Snakeplant) Tall, erect long leaves in green or varigated varieties. Cut leaves and lay flat to dry. Use as line material in arrangements.

Salsify: (Goatsbeard or Puffball) Found along the roadside. Pick while still green and stand to open into light puffs. Pick up dried puffs and spray with plastic fixative. Use in contrived flowers or on a mobile.

Fig. 1-18 Rudbeckia—black-eyed Susan.

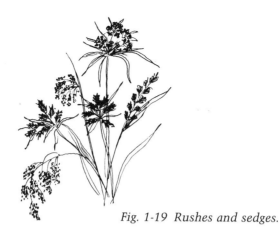

Fig. 1-19 Rushes and sedges.

Scotch Broom: Grows along the roadside in the south and north-west, cultivated garden plant elsewhere. Long stems, nearly leafless with yellow blossoms in the spring. Cut and dry in bunches, shaping in curves and circles. May be tied into a wreath while green and dried.

Strelitzia: (Bird-of-Paradise) Tropical plant available from florist. Flowers air dry but shrink. The rigid boat-like bracts dry and are useful in modern arrangements.

Sumac: Large shrub in the wilds or cultivated. Large red clusters of seeds appear in July. Various varieties available with the clusters different shades of red. Pick when color is brightest and hang to dry. Avoid the variety that has white berries, because it is poisonous and

Fig. 1-20 Sumac.

Fig. 1-21 Tansy.

causes skin rashes. The leaves turn gold and red in the fall and can be treated with glycerine mixture to preserve. Use seed pods in large arrangements at Christmas when red materials are needed.

Sunflower: Large yellow round flowers, either annual or perennial. Flowers may be dried in silica, or allow to set seeds. Remove center seeds and dry the empty seed cup for use in large arrangements of contrived flowers. Flowers from small varieties may be pressed for dried flower pictures. Foliage may be pressed or dried in silica.

Tansy: Originally cultivated for medicinal uses, now a wild garden plant throughout America. Similar in appearance to Achiella, but flowers develop into little yellow buttons. Pick at peak of color before they turn brown and hang to dry. Leaves dry easily and are heavy scented,

Fig. 1-22 Thistle.

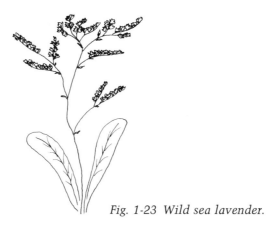

Fig. 1-23 Wild sea lavender.

very fragile when dry. May be added to potpourri or to herb wreaths when green.

Thistle: Numerous types with yellow, white, purple and red flowers. Pick flowers as color is beginning to show, using caution and heavy gloves. Remove stickers with a pair of pliers by running the pliers up and down the stem to scrape away the stickers. Hang to dry and flowers will continue to open. If picked too late the flowers will shatter.

Veronica: Long, narrow spikes of blue, white or pink flowers that open slowly along stem. Pick when partially open and hang to dry. Use in arrangements or on wreaths.

Wood Roses: Seed pods of the Hawaiian morning glory available from florists.

Wild Sea Lavender: *Do not pick from the shore line areas—this is a protected and endangered plant.* There are many garden species that are easy to grow and available from catalogues. The cultivated variety is showier and comes in different colors. Hang to dry and use as a light filler material in wreaths and arrangements.

Fall Dried Flowers and Berries

Barberry: Wild, thorny bush producing hanging clusters of yellow flowers in spring that turn into scarlet berries in the fall. Pick carefully, avoiding the sharp thorns and use in arrangements or wreaths. Excellent true red for decorations at Christmas.

Bayberry: Waxy gray-blue berries growing in thick clusters part way down the heavy stems. Remove leaves and top part of stem before drying. Stand or hang to dry for use in winter arrangements or wreaths. Bayberry is found along the seashore and was used for making candle wax by early settlers.

Black Alder: A variety of holly rather than a true alder. Bright red berries on long stems that remain throughout the winter. Excellent color for winter bouquets.

Bittersweet: A common vine producing bright yellow capsules that open revealing scarlet berries. May be a protected plant in some areas, so check with a local garden club before picking. Pick branches of the vine when the yellow capsules appear and before the red berries show.

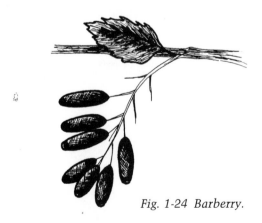

Fig. 1-24 Barberry.

Fig. 1-25 Bayberry.

Fig. 1-26 Black alder.

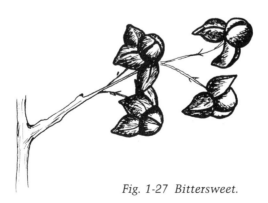

Fig. 1-27 Bittersweet.

29

Fig. 1-28 Burning bush.

If picked too late, the berries will shatter easily. Arrange vines on wreaths or arrangements while green and pliable.

Burning Bush: Berries resemble those of bittersweet, except the capsules enclosing red-orange berries are lobed and bright pink instead of yellow and round. Berries hang from twigs on long slender stems.

Chinese Bittersweet: Imported variety from Central and Western China. Berries completely cover vines in fall. Available from garden catalogues. Pick and use in the same way as common bittersweet.

Fire Thorn: (Pyracantha) Has orange, red, yellow or pink berries in late summer and early fall. Care must be taken to avoid the thorns when picking. Berries shrivel when dried.

Hazelnuts: Various varieties available. Pick while leafy coverings

Fig. 1-29-Fire thorn—pyracantha.

30

Fig. 1-30 Heavenly bamboo.

are plump and green, allowing to dry. The leafy coverings will open like fringed petals around the small nut.

Heavenly Bamboo: Bright red berries produced in the fall in large, cascading clusters. Cut when berries are red and hang to dry.

Highbush Cranberry: Bright red berries that dry well. Pick when fully red and hang to dry.

Milkweed Pod: Common roadside perennial. Petal-shaped pods may be picked green, or after opening and releasing fluffy seed centers. Use as is in arrangements or use pods for contrived flowers, gluing ends into pinecones. Small seeds may be glued into a Styrofoam ball for an unusual Christmas ornament.

Fig. 1-31 Milkweed pod.

Fig. 1-32 Privet

Okra: Listed as an annual herb, grown as a summer vegetable. Pick the long, ribbed pods before frost and air dry. Split open and the ends will curl into petals, or leave whole and use in arrangements or wreaths.

Privet: Berries ranging in colors of green or dark blue depending when branches are cut.

Strawberry Bush: Capsules are reddish pink and look like prickly strawberries until they split open and reveal the bright orange seeds inside.

Strawberry Corn: Small red corn kernels on a small, fat cob. Pull back husks and pin into petals for contrived flower.

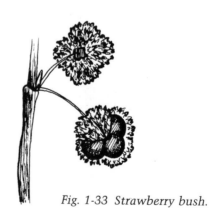

Fig. 1-33 Strawberry bush.

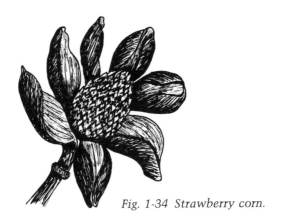

Fig. 1-34 Strawberry corn.

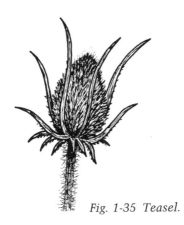

Fig. 1-35 Teasel.

Fig. 1-36 Yucca.

Sweet Gum: A deciduous tree producing brilliant red leaves in fall. Pick leaves before frost and treat in glycerine or air dry. Small brown, spiny pods are gathered and used with pinecones and other dried pods. Drill holes through pods and string on wire, or attach with glue gun.

Teasel: Tall, prickly stems with oval seed heads. Pick when dry on plant and remove stickers, rubbing with heavy gloves.

Unicorn Plant: (Devil's claw) Unique beaked seed pod that looks like a large insect. When dried can be used in many projects, such as wreaths or mobiles.

Yucca: Tall, tree-like roadside plant. White blooming spire in spring, pods forming on stems. Pick before frost and air dry. Pods may be left on spire, or removed and used in other projects.

Pine Cones, Nuts, and Seeds

Collect pine cones and seed pods in late summer and early fall after they have fallen to the ground and released their seeds. The seeds are the new generation of trees and feed for the birds, so practice conservation as you collect your cones. *Do not collect pine cones in public areas and state parks—it is against the law.*

Collect cones as soon as they fall from the tree; allow to open in a warm area and broadcast any seeds that fall out of the cones. Cones left on the ground begin to darken and deteriorate, becoming soft and unattractive.

Wash all cones in water, using a stiff wire brush to remove soil. To remove the pitch from fresh cones and add a shine, bake them on a large flat pan or cookie sheet at 200 F until the pitch melts. Do not over bake or the cones will turn too dark. The odor of baking cones is rather unpleasant, so try to do this on a day when you can open windows and doors to ventilate the house. Reserve the pans for this use, because the pitch will stain the pans and they should not be used for cooking. Baking the pine cones is also necessary for killing any small bugs. Many beautiful cone decorations have been ruined from bugs eating the cones. I was given a beautiful lei made from small wood roses. I packed it away in a box and when I went to wear the lei, I found it was destroyed by small bugs and I had a box of saw dust.

A mail-order source for pine cones is given in the Sources of Supplies in the back of the book.

Gather nuts and pods in later summer and early fall. Remove soil with a brush and hang pods to dry in a well-ventilated area. Bake nuts on a shallow pan in a 200 F oven for about 20 to 30 minutes to kill any insects that may be inside the nuts. Cool and store the nuts in metal cans with a few mothballs to discourage mice and other rodents. Nuts purchased from grocery stores are ready to use and do not need to be baked.

35

Wash all seeds in soap and water to remove any fleshy parts. Spread in a single layer on a flat pan and bake at 100 to 150F for 15 minutes to kill any insects and prevent germination of the seeds. Allow seeds to dry thoroughly before using and store in tightly covered cans to discourage mice. Save all seeds from pumpkins, squash, beans, watermelon, and other fruits and vegetables. Use on wall plaques or glue into small cones to make contrived flower shapes.

Wash fruit pits in soapy water and rinse to remove the fleshy parts. Spread to dry on a flat pan and bake at 100 to 150F for 30 minutes to kill insects. Store pits in tightly sealed cans with a few mothballs. Pits may be added to designs with a glue gun, or drill the end and add a wire. Clusters of pits make attractive additions to large pine cone wreaths. Save pits from avocados, peaches, plums, apricots, and dates.

How to Dry Flowers

Selecting Flowers for Drying

Listing the various flowers that are easily dried would fill pages. Basically trial and error will give you the amounts of flowers needed for any project. Knowing some of the things to look for will make it easier when you are just beginning. The color of a flower you choose to press will often indicate the success you will have. Most blue flowers retain their color well, so try delphiniums, forget-me-knots, morning glory and blue salvia. Most red flowers have excellent color retention, some fading to pink or an occasional shade of purple. Yellow and orange flowers seem to have the best color retention and last the longest without fading. My favorite little yellow wildflower is a buttercup. It is abundant and presses beautifully.

Individual blossoms from forsythia are good, as are the small yellow blossoms on a wild mullein stalk. Large flowers such as marigolds and coreopsis dry well if individual petals are removed and dried. A butterfly is made from four petals of the coreopsis in one of my designs. White

Fig. 1-37 Buttercup.

flowers are so necessary in a design. The addition of white seems to intensify all other colors. However, many white flowers do not dry well, and they may turn brown. Trial and error is often the only way to know. The amount of moisture in a flower petal may be a good clue as to whether it will dry or not.

Flowers like African violets and perennial phlox and English primroses are some that are very pretty but do not retain any of their color. They dry paper thin and colorless.

Drying Plants by Hanging

The most widely used method of drying plants is by picking and hanging the plants in a dark, dry area until dry. Many wild and cultivated herbs and plants retain their color and shape well by this simple method.

Choose an area such as a garage or attic; even a closet may be used for drying plants. The area being used must be dry and dark if possible. The most important thing is to remove the moisture from the flowers and stems as quickly as possible to prevent fading. Basements in most homes are not especially dry and may not be a suitable place for your drying efforts unless a dehumidifier is used during the humid summer months. Our home is always humid and we operate a dehumidifier in the basement to prevent my flowers and fabrics from molding. I hang my plants to dry in the garage from the rafters and have good success, and I store the more fragile flowers in boxes in the attic after they are dry.

The volume of materials collected from the roadsides and your garden can become overwhelming and create a storage problem. Collect small amounts of materials for personal use, and large amounts if you are working with a large group, making floral designs for a fund-raising event.

I made foraging trips at least two or three times a week during the growing season and carried home only the amount of materials I could prepare for drying in the next hour or two. The most important point is to get the plants ready for drying as soon as possible after picking. Pick only plants that are at their peak of color and freshness. All morning dew or rain must be gone and the plants completely dry. Strip away all leaves from the stems, leaving only the flower head for drying. If the leaves are left on the stems, the process of drying is slowed and the flowers will fade before they are dry.

Separate the plants into small bundles to avoid crowding of the flower heads. Tie the stems together with heavy string, tieing a loop on the end of the string. The stems will shrink as they dry, so the use of rubberbands is helpful and prevents the stems from sliding out of the bundle as they dry. Wired paper ties that are used in grocery stores are also excellent for binding bundles together.

Hang large, long-stemmed plants from the rafters, slipping the loops over nails spaced along the rafters. Do not crowd the plants, but allow air to circulate around the plants. Short-stemmed plants and flowers should be tied together with a small rubber band that has been attached to a coat hanger. The flowers may be left attached to the coat hangers until needed and hung in a dark closet after drying. Lavender, blue salvia, hydrangea blossoms, yarrow, chive blossoms, and many other flowers are easier to handle when attached to the coat hanger.

Drying time with all materials will depend upon the weather, and the size and length of the materials. Test for dryness before using in an arrangement. Large head flowers, such as Joe Pye weed will droop if arranged before the flowers are completely dry.

Curved stems may be desirable in some materials, such as wild grasses. Stand the long stems in a tall container and allow the heads to

Fig. 1-38 Attaching small clusters of flowers to a hanger using a rubberband. Hang to dry until ready to use.

fall in a graceful curve. A large pitcher is excellent for this when the stems are draped over the spout of the pitcher and allowed to dry. It is almost impossible to create curves in plant material after it is dry, so coax it as you prepare it for drying. Gentle curves add interest and remove the stiffness in a design caused by all straight stems. Various plants respond well to forcing curves by tying the stems in circles before hanging to dry. Pussy willow and broom are two examples.

Some flower heads such as strawflowers need extra support while drying to hold their flat shape. A special drying rack can be made from a wood box with a piece of mesh wire nailed to the top. The flowers are laid on the wire, with the stems placed through the wire. The heads are supported and the stems dry straight. Queen-Anne's-Lace, immortelles and globe amaranth are dried successfully this way. Many large annuals will dry nicely when the flower is supported this way; try button marigolds and mums. If the stem is soft after drying as with strawflowers, replace the stem with a wire before drying and suspend the flower in the drying rack.

Drying Plants in Sand

Sand is one type of drying agent that is used with some success. The sand must be very fine and free of debris or else the flower petals will be weighted down and crushed. Sand collected along the seashore is not suitable due to the high salt content. River sand is useful if sifted to remove large particles and washed and dried before using. All collected sands should be cleaned and dried before using for flower drying. A very fine silver sand used for seed planting may be purchased from a garden center and is excellent for use in flower drying. Flowers dried in sand have good color retention and have a matte finish.

Sand is heavy, so care must be taken as it is poured over the petals of flowers. Place sand around the outside of the flower first, supporting the petals before you begin to fill the top of the flower. All sand should be very dry before using as a drying agent. To dry sand, place the sand in a shallow container in a very low oven (250 F). The time needed to dry the sand depends upon the moisture content and amount of sand in the container. Stir the sand often to speed the drying process. Cool the sand before adding flowers or the hot sand will cook the flowers and they will be ruined immediately. It is not necessary to seal the top of a container when drying flowers in sand. Pour off the sand very slowly and carefully when the flowers are dry to prevent damaging the fragile petals with the heavy sand. The sand must be redried in the oven before it can be used again for drying more flowers.

Drying Flowers with Silica Gel

Silica gel is a white, moisture-absorbing granular substance and is the no. 1 choice for speed and success in drying plant materials. It is sold under various trade names at garden centers and florists. A mail-order source is offered in the Supply List.

Moisture is removed from plant material rapidly and the desiccant does not cake and crush even the most fragile flower. The shape and color of the flowers are retained as the flowers dry quickly. The length of time needed for each type of flower depends upon the size of the flower, the number of flowers in the same container and the size of the container. As a general rule, place all the same size and variety of flowers in the same container. The larger and heavier the flower head, the less you place in each container.

Select a firm container deep enough to allow a layer of silica gel on the bottom and at least $\frac{1}{2}$ inch over the flowers. The container should have a tight-fitting lid to prevent the accumulation of moisture from the atmosphere. A metal cookie tin works well, but so would any large plastic container with a tight lid.

Select flowers that are at their prime in color and petal firmness. Remove all of the stem, leaving a $\frac{1}{2}$ inch length below the flower head. Place the flower face up on the layer of silica gel, gently settling the flower on the surface of the gel. Fill the container with flowers, allowing space between each flower. The petals should not touch those of an adjacent flower. Slowly pour the silica gel around the base of each flower, supporting the petals. Fill the centers of each flower carefully with silica gel, being careful not to crush the petals. Try to retain the natural shape of the flower as closely as possible.

Mark the container with the date and contents and place the lid on the container and place in a dark, dry area, such as a closet. Check the process of drying after two to three days, depending upon the size of the flowers. Brush away the covering over a few petals and test for dryness. If the petals feel dry, slowly remove one of the flowers in the container to check the heavy center of the flower. The whole flower must be completely dry before removing from the container or the flower will droop and be unusable.

When it has been determined that all the flowers in the container are dry, slowly pour off the silica gel, being careful to not crush or break the brittle petals. Lift out each flower and shake the excess silica gel from the center of the flower. Use a soft paint brush to dust the petals if necessary to remove any particles of silica gel.

Store the dried flowers in large flat boxes in a dry area such as a closet or attic until ready to use in a design. Label the boxes as to color and flower type for ease in identifying the contents.

Drying Flowers in Silica Gel Using a Microwave Oven

Important—refer to your owner's manual for any special instructions for flower drying. Flowers placed in silica gel and dried in a microwave oven can be dried successfully in a very few minutes and even seconds, depending upon the size of the flowers.

1. Select flowers of the same size and type.

2. Use a glass container that will fit in the microwave oven, allowing space for a small dish containing 1 cup of water.

3. Fill the bottom of the container with a layer of silica gel. Place flowers on the surface and gently cover each flower with silica gel. Be careful to support the petals and not distort the natural shape of the flower.

4. Place the container of flowers and 1 cup of water in the microwave oven.

5. Approximate times for various flowers are listed below. All flowers are dried on the full power setting. Times are given for one or two flowers; add one half to one minute as needed for a container with more than three flowers. I used a large, 10-inch pie plate and was able to dry five or six roses.

Carnation: $2\frac{1}{2}$ to 3 minutes
Daffodil: $1\frac{1}{2}$ to 2 minutes
Dallias: 2 to 3 minutes depending on size
Rose: $1\frac{1}{2}$ to 2 minutes
Violets: $\frac{1}{2}$ to 1 minute
Zinnias: 2 to $2\frac{1}{2}$ minutes

Allow all flowers to stand in the silica gel until the glass container has cooled. The glass will get very hot and can burn your hands. Remove the container carefully from the microwave and set on a heat-resistant surface. Do not try to pour off the silica gel until it is cool. The silica gel cannot be reused until it has cooled completely.

Storing Silica-Dried Flowers

Remove the flowers from the cooled silica gel carefully and store them in large, flat boxes. Mark boxes with color and contents until ready to use in a project. Protect all silica-dried flowers from moisture. The prettiest daffodil will be instantly ruined if placed where it can collect moisture. Placing silica-dried flowers under glass and sealing the edges of the glass is a good idea. Place in large picture frames or under a dome glass jar for permanent display. Small arrangements are most successfully used during the winter months when household moisture is very low and winter is when the bright colors of the summer flowers are the most appreciated.

How to Press Flowers

One of the most effective ways of preserving the beauty of natural flowers is to dry the flower by pressing between sheets of newspaper or old telephone books. Each dried flower artist and naturalist has her own methods and recommendations for the type of materials to use. Some say that old catalogues do not absorb moisture due to the coated surface of the paper, yet I have used an old Sears catalogue for years with one sheet of facial tissue between the pages. Newspaper is excellent, yet some say the ink will smear and mark the flowers, but placing a layer of facial tissue on the newspaper prevents marking by the newspaper ink. Paper towels will transfer their waffle appearance to the petals.

My suggestion is start with what you have and begin to collect the beauty that is in bloom, picking and pressing and perfecting your methods as you collect your flowers. Many commercial flower presses are available with sheets of absorbent paper, the only drawback being that they are usually small and will not hold a large supply of flowers. It is quite easy to make a flower press of your own using two pieces of plywood and four small C-clamps. A stack of newspapers or the telephone book can be placed between the pieces of wood and the C-clamps attached at each corner and tightened.

Collecting Flowers for Pressing

Begin your collecting when the early morning dew has evaporated from the petals and foliage. If you choose to gather in the early morning hours when the flowers are fresh and damp, place the stems in warm water in the house and allow the flowers to air dry. Collecting along roadsides far from home requires carrying water with you and placing your freshly cut flowers in the water until you return home. Many wild flowers wilt as soon as they are cut and unless they are pressed in an old phone book immediately or given water, they will be unusable.

One of my garden club friends travels extensively and carries a small, old telephone book with her to collect flowers and foliage on her trips. You just never know when you are going to see something in bloom and wish you could have a few of the blossoms for your dried flower projects. A small basket with a pair of flower clippers or scissors, a jar of water, and a small phone book has become a standard addition to my car. (Gloves are also a good idea, just to protect you from stickers or the small bee that you may disturb.) As stated in the beginning of this book, pick only a few flowers from any one plant, cutting a small length of stem. Do not strip a plant of all the flowers and leaves. The plant will continue to grow and produce more flowers, as well as the seeds necessary for next year's plants. Always be a conservationist in all your collecting.

Pick the freshest blooms available for the best results. Dry or old flowers will shatter easily after drying. Pick small pieces of foliage and leaves, plus a few buds of each plant to add interest to your designs. Look for lacy ground covers and curly tendrils on plants and press. They make excellent additions to a picture, giving rhythm and movement to your design. The smallest and least noticeable plant may become your most valuable and treasured design material.

Pressing and Storing

Place your freshly picked material on the page in the telephone book press, filling one page at a time with the same type of flowers or leaves. Having the same thickness of flower heads or leaves on a page is important so that drying will occur evenly and uneven shrinking of petals will be prevented. Pick and press more than you may need, as some flowers may not look as nice as others after pressing. Place a half-inch of newspaper or pages of the book over the flowers and begin filling the top page with more flowers. If using an old phone book, start filling the book from the back, adding pages of flowers as they are collected each day. Place a marker in each page of flowers, writing the date and type of flower collected. This makes it easy to find the flowers you want and know how long they have been drying.

When pressing flowers with heavy centers, such as daisies, remove the stem and press separately. Stems on certain flowers will mark the flower and leave a ridge. Place the flower face down, placing as close together as possible on the page without touching. Remove individual flowers from large flower heads of hydrangea, geraniums and verbena and press each floret. One large flower head will yield pages of flowers. A red geranium flower presses beautifully and is an excellent source of red for designs. Many red flowers will turn purple when dry. White geraniums, however, turn brown.

Many flowers, such as roses, tulips and zinnias, are too thick to press as a whole flower. Carefully remove petals from the thick flower and press the petals. The petals may be used in designs individually or the flower reconstructed petal by petal after drying.

Place the papers or book in your C-clamps and wood, or add weight by placing under a stack of books, placing the book in a dry area. Weighing down the books or paper is the most important step. There must not be any air spaces around the material, as air will cause uneven drying, excessive shrinkage and discoloration of the flowers. Dampness causes flowers to turn brown, which is a waste of your time and flowers, so be sure your flowers are dry before pressing and they are placed in a dry area during pressing.

Experiment with all the flowers you see. Pick a few to begin with if you are not sure they will dry successfully. If you like the results, pick more and fill your pages. It takes approximately a week for most flowers to dry; the thickness of the flower determines how long it will take to dry. Most flower varieties bloom over a long period of time, so you have time to test most flowers before picking a large amount and finding that they don't press well and you have wasted your time and effort.

Your flowers may be left in the pages of the phone book or between the sheets of paper until needed. However, I prefer to remove my flowers and store them on plastic trays such as the ones from the grocery store. I place a facial tissue on the tray, add a layer of flowers and cover with another tissue. The tissues make it easy to remove a layer of flowers without damaging them. Fill the tray with layers of the same variety and color of flower. These can be stacked and stored easily, as they are so lightweight that they will not damage the pressed flowers. Your flower press or books are then free to press more flowers. Place the stacks of trays in paper bags and store in a dry area until ready to be used in pictures or other projects.

Color Washing Dried Flowers

Dried flowers may be arranged and used immediately after drying, but there are some designers that recommend taking the time to color wash the flowers and foliage to intensify colors and make the colors permanent. Dried flowers will fade in time, and color washing helps to prevent the fading. Color washing is not painting your flowers, it is the use of matching color applied in a thin film of color to intensive and brighten a flower. If a flower looks painted, it isn't being done right. Color wash one flower with a thin coat of paint and compare it to a natural flower. If you can't see the paint and the painted flower is a little brighter and more intense, you have the technique mastered. You have improved on nature a little and helped to retain her beauty for years to come.

It must be stated, however, that fading colors are not a detriment to a design. There are beautiful, ancient designs that are available in museums and private collections that have lost only the color of the flowers, but the designs remain intact for all to appreciate. A good quality watercolor paint and good brushes should be purchased if you intend to make large quantities of dried flower items. The better-quality paints are fade-proof and your designs will retain their color longer.

You will need various shades of yellow, green, blue, red, and white; a paint dish or other flat plastic or glass surface for mixing paints; brushes; tweezers; and paper towels. Place a flower or leaf on paper towels and begin selecting colors of paint, mixing small amounts to match as closely as possible the plant material. Thin the paints with water to create the "wash," and experiment with what seems right for the flower. The heavier the flower, the heavier the wash can be. Dip a clean brush in the paint and gently stroke the petals from the center outward, being careful not to tear or break a petal. If a petal comes loose, it can be replaced after drying with a little glue. Very thin flowers can not be washed as they will fall apart easily, so they are best left as they are. If too much color is added, go over each petal with a clean, wet brush and remove some of the paint. A light touch is what you are looking for.

A decision has to be made as to when you want to color wash your flowers—before you arrange them or after they are placed in your design. For the beginner it may be advisable to practice color washing a supply of flowers and then making a design. As you become proficient in designing and handling your materials, a picture or card can be designed, each flower removed from the design and color washed and then returned to its place in the design. The addition of the color wash to dried material has to be a personal choice and there is really no right or wrong. If you want your materials and designs to be entirely natural, then color wash is not for you.

Perhaps the thing most appealing about dried flowers is the texture and color that can be achieved. Nature has been captured in its finest. So much is missed when we look at a large tree or plant, as we see the whole plant or tree and not the individual parts. One of the best examples is a Japanese maple tree. It has exquisite leaves that are so beautiful on the tree, but dried they are even more wonderful.

Preserving Foliage and Flowers
in Glycerine

The use of glycerine for preserving foliage and flowers is a relatively new process in the world of flower arrangers. Most early flower arranging books do not mention this method of preserving plant materials, yet it is so easy and success is almost guaranteed for even the novice flower arranger. It requires a minimum of time to prepare the materials, and nature does the rest.

Glycerine is the most popular substance used for preserving plants, but a mixture of water and antifreeze is also effective. In this discussion I will be referring to glycerine as the substance used for preserving, but antifreeze may be substituted. Glycerine is obtainable from a drug store and is expensive; antifreeze is less expensive and easily found in automotive stores. Ready-to-use glycerine is available from Activa Products, Inc. (see Sources of Supplies).

The glycerine solution is carried through the stems of the plants, into the veins of the leaves, and out into the tissues of the leaves. Moisture is replaced by the glycerine and the leaf is permanently preserved in its natural shape. The veins on the back of the leaf will begin to darken and indicate the progress of the solution through the leaf. As the glycerine solution progresses through the stems and leaves, the color of the leaves will begin to change. Color changes range from dark green through the shades of beige to dark brown. The type and age of the foliage determines the colors achieved. Often the same type foliage will turn a different shade of brown if preserved at different times during the growing season. The pale green foliage of the beech tree will turn a light olive green, yet the yellow fall foliage of the same tree will turn a beautiful bronze. The colors of the foliage after treatment with an antifreeze solution are not as deep or rich as those of the glycerine-treated materials.

49

When flowers and foliage are preserved with a glycerine mixture, the foliage retains its flexibility, is pliable to the touch and can be used out of water for years. It can be cleaned in warm water and dried, or wiped clean with a damp cloth.

The age of the leaves being preserved is very important. Foliage that is too young is not developed enough for the glycerine solution to penetrate the veins, and the top-most leaves on a branch will wilt before preserving. Foliage that is too old and tough cannot absorb the mixture. Picking flowers and foliage in mid-season will give the best results, but do try at different times of the year to see what may happen. Foliage that is just beginning to change color in early fall can be preserved and retain the beautiful yellows and reds. Pick early, just as the color has covered the foliage, but not after the foliage has started to dry, or else the leaves will fall and not soak up the solution. Experiment with everything you see, picking a small amount at first to see if you get good results, then go back and pick as much as you need for your arrangement.

Many varieties of plants with berries will preserve well. Pick berried branches when the berries are full and plump and allow leaves to soak up the solution of glycerine and water. The berries will change a little and there may be a little shrinkage, but the berries will remain attached to the stems.

Branches of junipers and conifers will preserve easily and the blue berries on some varieties will retain their pretty colors. The foliage may turn a soft brown, but some I processed retained the blue-green color of their natural state. Sprays of heather will retain the small needle-like foliage and small flowers that provide the soft lacy beauty of this foliage. It is very fragile when air dried, so preserving this foliage with glycerine is a definite advantage.

Experiment with every foliage you have, even the house plants. Or purchase foliage from your local florist and see what results you get. Save the leaves from your bouquets of roses and other flowers and preserve for use in future arrangements. Preserved foliage may be added to fresh flower arrangements without damaging the preserved foliage. Dip the ends of the preserved foliage into clear nail polish, varnish, or melted wax to seal the ends. This prevents the absorption of water that may cause mold to develop on the preserved foliage.

The preserving solution is made up of one part glycerine to two parts boiling water. Glycerine will "float" in the water and the hot water helps to disperse the glycerine evenly in the water. The hot water is also necessary to increase the uptake of the solution by the plant. Some instruction books recommend adding bleach to the solution to prevent mold from developing on the foliage after processing, but if the foliage is stored in a dry area there shouldn't be a problem with mold.

Do not discard leftover solution. It can be used over and over by adding more glycerine and water. The darkening of the solution does not affect the results of new material. Strain the solution if a large amount of debris has collected. Reheat the solution each time new material is added to the solution to increase absorption.

Choose containers of suitable height to the material being preserved. Generally a container with a narrow opening, such as a milk bottle or quart mayonnaise jar is best. The weight of the jar will support heavy stems and there will be little evaporation of the solution. Fill the jar with the solution to a depth of 4 to 6 inches, or the amount needed to cover the ends of the stems. Short clusters of leaves, such as rhododendron, need a shorter container and the appropriate amount of solution.

Clean all materials by washing under running water and trim away broken or insect-damaged leaves. It is a waste of the glycerine to preserve less than perfect materials. Many books recommend that the leaves be coated with the solution to speed absorption and preserving, but I found I had continuous success by placing fresh material in the solution immediately after picking. Crush at least three inches of the stems with a hammer to break the bark and shred the center of the stems. This will ensure the absorption of the liquid quickly and prevent wilting of the top leaves before they are preserved. Place the stems into the solution, making sure the shredded stems are covered. Do not overcrowd the materials in a container, making sure there is enough solution to support the amount of material being preserved.

Place the containers in a well-ventilated, dry area to prevent possible molding of the material. Placing the container in bright sunshine results in unusually pale colors as the sun tends to bleach the leaves as they preserve. Check to be sure enough solution is in the container to cover the stems of the material. Preserving in a dark, dry area will produce different colors in the same type of materials.

The foliage will begin to show a change of color in a few days. The veins on the back of the leaves will show how much of the solution is being absorbed. There isn't a specific amount of time that can be given for preserving each type of foliage. Preserving can take from one week to as much as one month depending upon the size of material in the container and the color that is to be achieved. The longer a material is left in the solution, the darker will be the color. As soon as the solution has reached the tip of the branch and the leaves feel leathery, the branches may be removed from the solution. Wipe off the excess solution from the stems and leaves and store in a box in a dry area until needed for an arrangement.

Certain types of vines and foliage preserve better if they are submerged in the solution. Large leaves of ivy, hosta, maple leaves and certain ground covers such as periwinkle preserve easily this way. Small cuttings of ivy may be placed in a round container and will retain the curves after preserving—a definite plus to the flower arranger that likes to use curved lines. Cut individual leaves from a branch and clean as for larger branches. Place in a container and cover with the glycerine solution. If the leaves try to float, use a glass plate or a similar object to hold the materials under the solution. Materials preserved by submerging tend to remain dark green, but in time will turn brown. The large ivy leaves used in the projects for the Christmas room were submerged in the solution to preserve.

Do not discard the solution, but cover tightly with a lid and save until you have foliage to preserve.

Here's a partial list of foliage that preserve well in glycerine:

Andromeda	Goldenrod
Barberry	Gypsophila
Beech	Hydrangea
Boxwood	Holly
Birch	Hosta
Canna	Iris
Cotoneaster	Juniper
Crabapple	Laurel
Dogwood (protected plant in some areas)	Lemon
Eucalyptus	Magnolia
Euonymus	Maple
English ivy	Mountain ash
Forsythia	Oak
Galax	Peony
	Periwinkle

Philodendron
Pine
Plum
Poplar
Pachysandra
Flowering quince
Queen-Anne's-Lace
Redwood
Rhododendron
Russian olive

Rubber plant
Spirea
Sweet gum
Sweet fern
Sumac
Ti
Viburnum
Wiegela
Yucca

As this is only a partial list of all the plants available, pick and try everything you see. As a general rule, the heavier the leaves, the better success you will have in preserving with glycerine solution.

Making Contrived Flowers

Corn Husk Flowers

Purchase or collect large, wide corn husks. Make flowers following the steps below, using the husks in their natural colors or use commercial fabric dye to achieve the color desired.

1. To dye corn husks: Purchase Rit dye in liquid or powder form and prepare a concentrated solution filling a wide-mouthed quart canning jar one-half full. Use boiling water and add 1 tablespoon of glycerine to the jar. The glycerine will soften the corn husks and make them easier to shape into flowers. Place the corn husks into the liquid, packing the jar as tightly as possible with husks to prevent their floating in the liquid. Do not be concerned if the ends of the husks stick up above the top of the jar. Place the end of the husk that was attached to the corn cob at the top of the jar. The corn husks will absorb the dye and the exposed corn husks will be streaked with dye in an interesting fashion. Allow corn husks to remain in the dye solution until the desired color is achieved. Remove the husks and allow the excess dye to drain back into the jar. Do not discard the dye; put a lid on the jar and store in a cool spot. Open out each corn husk and allow to dry on paper towels.

2. Large corn husk flower: Select one large corn husk and cut a 6-inch length of husk, reserving the end that is not completely dyed. This piece will be used in another style of flower. Refer to Fig. 1-41 and fold the husk accordian style and round the ends or cut to a point. Open the corn husk out flat and insert a piece of wire in and out through the center of the husk (Fig. 1-42). Fold the corn husk in half over the wire and gently gather the corn husk along the wire (Fig. 1-43). Twist the wire ends together tightly as close to the corn husks as possible. Insert a dried flower seed head in the center of the corn husks and twist the wires around the stem (Fig. 1-44). Cover the wires and stem with brown

Fig. 10 Fall foliage and bee balm seed heads on an excelsior wreath, with strawberry corn and dried gourd accent.

Fig. 11 Christmas room with wreath, mantel swags, Colonial fruit cone, topiary centerpiece, and ornamented tree. Table decorations designed by Shirley Girioni.

Fig. 12 Summer wreath of goldenrod and flowers. Photographed at The Thomas Griswold House, Guilford, CT.

Fig. 13 Clockwise from left: heart-shaped straw wreath with hydrangea and strawflowers, designed by Elenore Hartman; hydrangea and ribbon wreath on a wire frame; artemesia heart with strawflowers on wire frame, by Elenore Hartman.

Fig. 16 Overleaf: *Festive winter doorway with heart wreath and bouquets in white wicker baskets. Photographed at A Summer Place, Guilford, CT.*

Fig. 14 *Author's prize-winning arrangement of protea, strelitzia, and abalone shell in a porthole window. Photographed at the home of Mr. and Mrs. John English.*

Fig. 15 **From left:** *hydrangea wreath with strawflowers, designed by Elenore Hartman; elegant spray of artemesia, celosia, and globe thistle; hydrangea wreath with globe amaranth, pearly everlasting, and suveroni, designed by Elenore Hartman.*

Fig. 1-39 Contrived flowers: Pine cones with milkweed pods; dyed corn husks formed around seed heads; lunaria petals glued into a teasel.

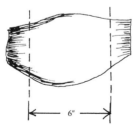

6″

Fig. 1-40 Cut corn husk on dotted lines for contrived flowers. Reserve base end after dyeing corn husk for making a small flower.

Fig. 1-41 *Fold corn husk into ¾ inch widths, accordian style. Trim ends in a curve with scissors.*

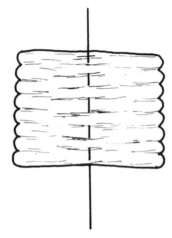

Fig. 1-42 *Weave a piece of wire in and out through the center of the corn husk.*

Fig. 1-43 *Fold the corn husk over the wire and gather the corn husk on the wire.*

florist tape. Any number of dried seed heads may be used as flower centers. The large sunflowers pictured in the bittersweet arrangement (Fig. 2-23) have seed heads from bee balm. Some of the red flower petals are still attached to the seed head, adding interest to the center of the flower. The corn husks may be cupped up around the seed head, or left flat, exposing the center. More than one piece of corn husk may be used in a flower to make as large and full a flower as you desire.

Fig. 1-44 Twist ends of wire together as close as possible to the corn husk. Pull corn husk apart into petals or leave in one piece. Insert large seed head in center and tape wire and stem with florist tape.

3. Small corn husk flowers: The reserved pieces cut from the dyed corn husks above are gathered onto a piece of wire, running the wire through the bottom edge of the husk. Pull the wire up tightly and insert a dried seed head into the center of the flower, cupping the corn husk up around the center. Wind the wire ends around the stem and cover the stem with brown florist tape.

4. Star-shaped corn husk flowers: Select five to six small- to medium-width pieces of corn husk and cut all to the same length, depending upon how large a flower you wish to make. Hold the pieces together and trim one end in a curve or to a point to make a petal shape. Gather the straight end of each petal and wrap with a small piece of

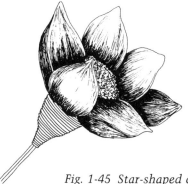

Fig. 1-45 Star-shaped corn husk flower.

Fig. 1-46 Trim the ends of five to six medium-wide corn husks into a point.

Fig. 1-47 Gather the end of each corn husk and wrap with fine florist wire. Attach each petal at the base of a large seed head with wire. Cover stem and wires with florist tape.

wire. Select a seed head for a center and wire each petal around the base of the seed head. Cover the wire and stem with brown florist tape.

Lunaria (Money Plant) Flowers

1. Lunaria and teasel flowers: Cut individual petals from a branch of lunaria. Remove the stickers from the stem of the teasel. The teasel may be spray-painted or left in it's natural beige color. Gently bend back the long, curved stems at the base of the teasel. Dip the cut end of a lunaria petal into white craft glue and insert the petal at the base of the teasel, pushing the petal into the teasel head. Continue inserting petals around the base of the teasel, adding as many rows of petals as desired. The top of the teasel may be left exposed as a flower center, or the petals can completely cover the teasel.

2. Agapanthus (lily of the Nile) dried flower heads are very attractive if filled with lunaria petals. Remove any dried flower petals from the seed head. Spray-paint the seed head white, a color, or leave natural. Glue the lunaria petals around the center of the dried head between the dried spokes of the agapanthus.

Pine Cone Flowers

1. Pine cone stars: Pick and open milkweed pods in the early fall. Remove the silky seed heads and trim off the end of each pod. Select a small, flat pine cone such as a Scotch pine or pinyon pine. Each of these pine cones are strong and tough and will support the large milkweed pod without breaking the pine cone. Select five milkweed pods of equal size and length. The pine cone and pods may be sprayed white, colors, or left in their natural colors. Dip the flat end of the pod in glue and insert around the bottom row of petals on the pine cone. Allow the glue to dry before handling the flower. Interesting flowers can be made using milkweed pods that are tightly curled; the flower resembles a large tulip. The milkweed pods may be trimmed and shaped with scissors into any shape of petal, creating a different flower each time. Experiment with different varieties of pine cones or seed pods as the center.

2. Pine cone flowers: Any number of flower shapes can be made using small pine cones as the center and adding dried grass heads or flowers around the pine cone. Select a small, flat rosette-type pine cone, such as a Norway flower, or cut off the top of a larger cone using the top as a flower center. Fill in the petals of the pine cone with clusters of grasses, baby's breath, dried flowers, or any interesting material, creating your own special flower.

Chinese Lantern Flowers

The large orange pods of the Chinese lantern may be opened by cutting along the ribs with scissors, forming petals around the bright red berry center. If you want the flower to open out flat, it will be necessary to hold the petals open with a small piece of tissue paper cupped around the berry until the petals dry.

PART TWO

Projects for All Seasons

Spring Specialties

Pressed Flower Wyndo-Card

Wyndo-Card
Clear plastic Contac paper
Small pressed flowers: violets, violas, small ferns, etc.
1 sheet colored stationery
Aleene's Designer Tacky Glue
Tweezers, scissors, paper

Select small pressed flowers suitable for the opening on the Wyndo-Card. Open card and draw around oval opening on a separate piece of paper. Place flowers on this piece of paper in a pleasing design and transfer to the colored stationery after design is finished.

Choose a medium-weight stationery with a background color that complements the colors of the flowers used in the design. Cut the stationery to fit inside the card and transfer the flower design to the stationery using tweezers.

Place a small amount of glue on the back of the flowers and carefully position them on the stationery. Set aside and allow glue to dry before covering with Contac paper. Cut a piece of Contac paper to fit the card plus $\frac{1}{4}$ inch on all sides. Remove paper backing and position over card, starting at top and smoothing carefully over flowers. Trim edges even with card. Insert or glue into Wyndo-Card.

Fig. 2-1 Spring dried flowers on note cards and book mark. The small "butterflies" are made from coreopsis petals.

Pressed Flower Book Mark

Colored paper
White paper
Narrow ribbon
Pinking shears
Contac paper
Aleene's Designer Tacky Glue
Small pressed flowers

Cut a 2-inch-by-5-inch strip of colored paper using pinking shears. Cut white paper to fit in center, allowing $\frac{3}{8}$ inch border around the sides and bottom and 1 inch at top. Punch a hole in the top and tie the ribbon in the hole. Glue small flowers to the paper, cover with Contac, and glue the finished design to the center of the book mark.

Pressed Flower Card

Envelopes
Contrasting colored stationery
Lace trims
Pressed flowers to complement colored stationery
Aleene's Designer Tacky Glue
Contac paper
Pinking shears, tweezers

This card is made from a variety of papers and is a good use for leftover envelopes and cards that don't match. Select three different colors of stationery. Cut one piece of paper to fit inside the envelope; cut the second piece $\frac{1}{4}$ inch smaller and glue to the center of the first piece of paper. Cut the third piece of paper $\frac{1}{4}$ inch smaller than the second piece. Select small flowers for the design and position them on a piece of scrap paper with tweezers. To make a small butterfly, select four petals from a coreopsis flower, two small and two slightly larger. Glue the petals in shape of wings, with the larger petals on the bottom and the small petals on the top of the wings. Select a small leaf or other material for the body, adding tiny curved stems for antennae.

Cover the finished design with Contac. Trim the edges of the design with pinking shears and glue to the center of the second card. Glue this to the larger card and trim the edges with lace as shown in Fig. 2-1.

Framed Pressed Flowers

Small oval frames approximately 4 inches by 6 inches
Colored paper, velvet fabric, rice paper, etc.
Small pressed flowers and foliage
Aleene's Designer Tacky Glue
Tweezers, scissors, Contac paper

Remove the backing from the picture frame and, using the paper insert as a pattern, cut a piece of colored paper or fabric the same size. Glue the paper or fabric to the frame backing and put aside. Select small pressed flowers that complement the background and develop your design on a piece of paper. Transfer the design to the background using tweezers, gluing the flowers in place. Cover the design with Contac if the frame does not have a piece of glass. Reassemble the picture frame.

Fig. 2-2 Pressed flowers in oval frames, preserving the beauty of spring.

Napkin Ring and Place Card

Medium-weight colored paper
Pressed flowers to complement table setting
Contac paper
Narrow pregathered lace, $\frac{1}{2}$ yard for each napkin ring
Glue, tweezers, scissors

For the napkin rings, cut strips of colored paper $2\frac{1}{2}$ inches by 8 inches. Glue small flowers to the center of the strip. Cut Contac to fit the paper and smooth over the design. Glue lace to the back edges of the paper and glue the ends of the paper together to form a ring.

For the place card, cut a piece of colored paper 4 inches by 5 inches. Fold paper in half, matching the 5 inch edges. Glue small pressed flowers in the left-hand corner below the fold. Cover with Contac. Names may be written with a black felt marker. Lace may be added if desired.

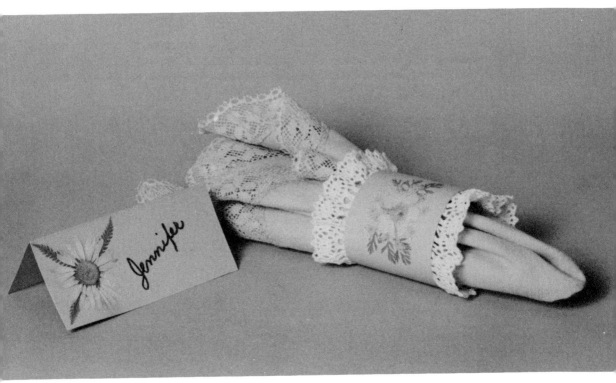

Fig. 2-3 Pressed flowers on napkin ring and place card.

Dried Flower Sun Catcher

2 6-inch glass disks from Houston Art and Frame Co.
1 yard satin picot ribbon, $\frac{1}{4}$ inch wide
Small piece Oasis
Sphagnum moss
Quick Grab glue
Small dried flowers, leaves, and ferns

Cut a small piece of Oasis about 2 inches long by 1 inch high and $\frac{1}{2}$ inch thick. Cover Oasis with thin layer of moss. Place Oasis at lower edge of one glass disk, positioning above lower edge about 1/2 inch. Glue to glass with a small amount of clear-drying glue such as Quick Grab by 3C Company. Arrange small flowers and foliage in the base, placing foliage in the center and flowers on both sides so that they can be seen when disks are glued together. Glue the second disk over design. Glue ribbon around the edges, and add a long loop of ribbon for hanging. Tie two small ribbon bows and glue over the ends of the loop.

Fig. 2-4 Wild flowers sealed between two glass circles and finished with picot ribbon,

Heart and Oval Boxes with Flowers

Small heart-shaped or oval chipwood boxes
$\frac{1}{2}$ yard craft ribbon
Lace
Small dried flowers
Glue, scissors, tweezers

Cut craft ribbon to fit sides and top of boxes. Spread an even coating of glue on the boxes and smooth the ribbon in place. Glue lace around top edge of lids. Glue small dried flowers to center. You may wish to paint the insides of the boxes or line with ribbon before decorating outside.

Fig. 2-6 Oval and heart-shaped chipwood boxes are covered with craft ribbon and the tops decorated with small dried flowers and lace.

Apothecary Jar and Plastic Coaster Set

Glass apothecary jar and/or plastic coaster set
Right-On from Artis, Inc.
Pressed flowers
Paint brush or sponge brush
Aleene's Designer Tacky Glue
Tweezers

Right-On is a new clear coating available at craft stores. It is odorless and gives a crystal-clear protective film on any surface. Use the gloss formula for this project. Select small flowers and foliage such as ferns and arrange on a piece of paper before applying to glass surface. Wash and dry the glass surface before applying flowers.

Apply a very small amount of glue on the back of the ferns and place ferns on the glass. Gently curve the ferns around the sides of the apothecary jar. If the stems break, add a little glue and repair. Try not to have glue showing around dried materials. Add flowers to center of design.

Lay the jar down on the table and support the sides so that the jar is stable and won't roll around as you are adding the protective coating. Pour a small amount of Right-On into a small cup. Dip brush into cup and completely fill brush; position brush over dried material and allow the liquid to flow over the flowers and ferns. Do not brush, but flood with liquid (the flowers may tear and break if you try to brush on the liquid). Completely flood the design, allowing the liquid to flow beyond the design area and seal edges of flowers. The liquid will dry clear and seal flowers to the glass so that the glass can be washed carefully when soiled or dusty.

Follow basic directions above and apply pressed flowers to the front of the plastic coaster stand as shown in Fig. 2-7. Try adding pressed flowers to other glass and plastic surfaces such as sun catchers, lamp bases, and lamp shades.

Fig. 2-7 *Pressed flowers sealed to a glass apothecary jar and plastic coaster set.*

Twig Heart Set

Small, medium, and large twig hearts from Lamrite's
Picot satin ribbon, $\frac{1}{4}$ inch to $\frac{3}{8}$ inch wide
Small dried flowers and baby's breath
Small package lavender potpourri
White nylon organdy
Glue or glue gun
Brown florist tape
Cardboard
Scissors, pinking shears
Wire, wire cutters

Small heart: Starting at center top of heart, wind $\frac{1}{4}$ inch-wide ribbon around heart, gluing ends at back of heart. Make small clusters of dried flowers and baby's breath and tape ends together with brown florist tape. Glue the clusters to wreath, positioning clusters between the ribbons. Cut a 9-inch length of ribbon and fold into a loop. Glue loop to center top of wreath. Tie remaining ribbon into a small bow and glue to top of wreath.

To make potpourri sachet for wreath: Trace heart pattern onto lightweight cardboard and cut out. Cut out two hearts from white organdy using pinking shears to prevent edges from fraying. Pin and sew around edges of heart on the seam line. Leave a 2-inch opening along one side of heart. Fill heart with lavender potpourri and stitch closed. Glue potpourri heart to back of twig wreath using glue gun or Aleene's Designer Tacky Glue. Allow to dry and hang in closet or on Christmas Tree.

Medium heart: Wind ribbon evenly around wreath, gluing ends at top center on back of wreath. Cut a 10-inch length of ribbon and fold into a loop; glue loop to center top of wreath. Fold ribbon into a bow with three loops on each side. Wire bow in center and glue to top of wreath. Hold together small clusters of dried flowers and tape ends together with brown florist tape. Make two clusters the same size and glue to sides of wreath. Fold ribbon into three small loops and glue under the flower clusters. Make a round cluster of flowers and glue to center of ribbon bow on top of wreath.

Large heart: Wind ribbon around wreath, gluing ends to center top on back of wreath. Make six small clusters of dried flowers, taping ends together with florist tape. Evenly space three clusters on each side of

Fig. 2-8 Twig heart set from Lamrite's decorated with ribbons and dried flowers. The small wreath has potpourri sealed in organdy fabric.

wreath and glue in place. Make a large cluster of the same flowers and glue to the bottom of the wreath. Cut ribbon into 9-inch lengths and tie into bows; make six bows and glue bows to wreath below clusters of flowers. Tie remaining ribbon into large bow and glue to top center of wreath. Add a loop of wire to back of wreath.

Flowered Potpourri Ball

Wire kissing ball from K.I.T.I.
4 yards white craft pearls from Lamrite's
2 yards white satin ribbon, ⅛ inch wide
¼ yard yellow nylon tubing from MPR Assoc.
White-flocked gyp and blue gypsy grass from Lamrite's
Yellow statice
Small package potpourri
White florist tape
Glue gun or glue

Cover each wire of kissing ball with white floral tape. Break statice, blue gypsy grass and white gyp into small pieces about 2 inches long. Make small clusters starting with white gyp, adding blue gypsy grass below the gyp and yellow statice at the bottom. Tape ends of all materials together with white floral tape. It will take approximately four small clusters to cover each segment of the wire kissing ball, or 48 clusters in all. Starting at the top of the ball, attach the flower clusters to the wire rings using the floral tape. Add each cluster so that the white gyp covers the ends of the previous cluster.

Glue one end of the craft pearls to the center top of the ball and wind the pearls loosely around the flower clusters. Glue ends of the pearls at the top and bottom of the ball.

To make the potpourri ball: Wire or tie one end of the yellow nylon tubing and turn the tubing inside out. Place the closed end inside the kissing ball and glue to the bottom of the kissing ball. Fill the nylon tubing with potpourri, stretching the nylon to fill the center of the kissing ring. Tie or wire the top opening and trim away excess fabric, leaving a ½ inch top on the fabric. Glue the top of the potpourri ball to the underside of the kissing ball, making the potpourri ball secure within the kissing ball.

Cut one 10-inch length of ribbon and put aside. Loop remaining ribbon together into loops about 3 inches long, and wire the center of the loops. Glue the loops to the top of the kissing ball. Loop remaining pearls together and glue to the center of the ribbon loops. Fold the 10-inch piece of ribbon into a loop and glue to the center of the pearls.

Potpourri ball may be hung in a closet or bathroom, where the moist air will release the aroma of the potpourri. Add fragrant oils to revive the potpourri as needed.

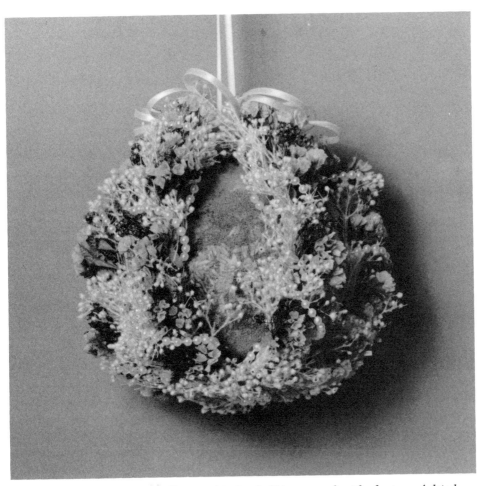

Fig. 2-9 Potpourri kissing ball: Wire kissing ball is covered with clusters of dried flowers and holds potpourri.

Straw Hat Candle Ring

12-inch flat straw hat from Lamrite's
1 yard white lace, 2 inches wide
3 yards white satin picot ribbon
2 yards blue lace-edged craft ribbon, 2 inches wide
White statice, red achillea (dries lavender/pink)
White-flocked gyp and blue gypsy grass from Lamrite's
White florist tape
Glue gun or glue
Large blue candle

Cover rim of straw hat with white lace, gluing edge of lace around crown of hat. Gather one edge of blue ribbon to fit around rim of hat and glue over the white lace around crown of hat.

Break dried flowers into small pieces. Starting with white-flocked gyp, add blue gypsy grass, white statice, and achillea to make small clusters. Tape ends together with white florist tape. Repeat clusters, making as many as you need to cover rim of hat (12 to 13 clusters).

Cut white picot ribbon into 9-inch lengths and fold into a cluster of three small loops. Tape loops to end of each flower cluster using white florist tape. Glue each ribbon-trimmed flower cluster around the rim of the hat, placing the clusters close together and covering the ends of the previous cluster.

To use as a candle ring, press down on the center of the straw hat to make an indentation. Select a small glass dish that will fit within the indentation and place candle in dish.

Fig. 2-10 Straw hat candle ring, decorated with ribbons and flower clusters.

Straw Hat Door Decoration

12-inch straw hat from Lamrite's
1 yard white lace, 2 inches wide
2½ yards print lace-edged craft ribbon
3 yards pink picot ribbon, ⅛ inch wide
Lavender and white statice
Green and lavender gypsy grass and stardust gyp from Lamrite's
Dried rosebuds
Glue
White florist tape

Refer to Candle ring instructions (p.76) and cover rim of hat with lace and ribbon. Make ten clusters of dried flowers starting with stardust gyp, adding lavender and green gypsy grass and lavender and white statice. Tape ends of dried materials together with florist tape. Cut picot ribbon into 9-inch lengths and fold into clusters of three loops each. Tape clusters of ribbon to base of each dried flower cluster. Glue flower clusters to rim of hat, overlapping to cover taped ends. There will be a 4-inch space on rim of hat not covered with flowers. Tie print ribbon into a bow and glue to open space. Glue rosebuds to center of bow and tuck a few into dried flowers around rim.

Fig. 2-11 Straw hat door decoration, with clusters of dried flowers and rose buds.

Spring Wreath of Clover and Wild Grasses

14-inch straw wreath from Lamrite's
Wild clover blossoms, pink and white ajuga, purple Siberian iris,
    snow-in-summer (cerastium)
Fresh green grasses
Florist picks

This spring wreath is shown in Color Fig. 4. One of the easiest ways to make a natural wreath is to use a straw wreath as the base. Straw wreaths are available from garden centers and craft stores. If not available in your area, write to Lamrite's.

Pick a large supply of roadside grasses in early spring and bring them home to make the wreath. Grasses will shrink as they dry, so pick more than seems necessary. Pick the grasses at different stages during the growing season for different uses and appearance. This wreath is made from grasses picked early in the season while the grass heads are tightly closed so that there will be a minimum of shedding after the grasses are dry. The fully opened and fluffy heads of grasses are more fragile and shatter as they are handled, but are excellent as fillers for wreaths or arrangements.

Grasses may be cut and dried in large bunches by hanging upside down in a dry area and used for the wreath after drying. However I find it easier to pick my grasses while they are green and make my wreaths with the fresh grasses.

Cut the grasses leaving a 4- to 5-inch length of stem and hold six to eight together and stagger the height of the grass heads in the bunch. If the grass stems are heavy and strong, the bunches may be added to the straw wreath by pushing the stems into the base. As the grasses dry, some of the pieces may fall out, but just push them back into the straw. This method is fast and easy. When you are ready to change the materials on the straw base, just pull everything out and start over. A more secure wreath can be made if the grass bunches are wired to a florist pick and the picks inserted into the straw base.

Cover the straw base completely with bunches of grass, placing the bunches close together to make a very full green wreath. As the materials dry, the colors will soften and there will be shrinkage, so have a reserve of the grasses and fill in the base as needed.

Decorate the wreath with wild clover and other materials in bloom and enjoy the colors and scents of the fresh material. It is easier to add the flowers to a full wreath of this type if the flower stems are wired to a florist pick and inserted into the straw.

Pick clover blossoms when the color is the brightest for the best color retention. Clover will fade and turn a soft shade of brown, but if you want to retain the lavender color permanently the flower heads will need to be dried in silica gel. Remove the leaves at each side of the clover blossom. The leaves dry nicely on the stems and add volume to the wreath, but the side leaves tend to curl around the clover head and hide the color.

Hold together four clover blossoms and two or three sprigs of snow-in-summer, and wire to a florist pick. Cover the front of the wreath with these clusters. Leave an opening at the top of the wreath for a ribbon bow.

Wire three stems of pink ajuga to a florist pick and insert into the wreath, placing ajuga clusters on the inside and outside of the clover clusters. Blue and white ajuga may also be used since they dry nicely.

Pick the Siberian iris stems when the first flower has opened and the flower is fresh. Each stem has one to two more buds on the stem and the buds will dry and retain the dark purple color. Hang the iris stems to dry; do not crowd the flowers or they will be flat. Add to the grass wreath after the flowers are completely dry.

As spring changes into summer, add other blooming flowers to the wreath changing colors as the flowers become available. Do not discard the dried materials, but pack the clusters away in a box for a future design or wreath. Clover and grasses are so abundant, however, that you don't need to save them, but if you have taken the time to dry your clover in silica gel, then definitely save the clover for future projects.

Summer's Blossoms

Summer Wreath of Goldenrod and Flowers

14-inch straw wreath from Lamrite's
Large amount of goldenrod, flower heads only
Perennial sunflower (helianthus), monarda (bee balm or bergamot),
    crested celosia (red), red salvia, Queen-Anne's-lace, white yarrow,
    achillea
Fern pins, floral picks
Yellow ribbon, chenille stem

This cheery yellow wreath is shown in Color Fig. 12. Goldenrod blooms abundantly from early June, throughout the summer and into fall, making it an excellent choice as base material for a lovely wreath. The trick to using goldenrod is pick it early, just as the small flowers begin to open at the base of the flower head. The heads will continue to open partially and intensify in color. Fully opened heads of goldenrod shatter easily and are messy. When you have located a supply of goldenrod, pick the flower heads that are ready and return often to the same areas for more blossoms. Picking only the flower heads will encourage the stems to produce side shoots and more flower heads for reseeding. To conserve nature's beauty, never overpick an area. (If you plan to use the flowers in an arrangement, then pick the full length stem.) Tie the flower heads or stems together in small bunches and hang to dry, or make the wreath with the fresh material.

If at all possible work outside or in the garage, as you will have carried home many small creatures that may be unwelcome in your home. Working outside helps to eliminate most of them so that the wreaths can be used inside. Cover your work area with newspaper or a large sheet of plastic (old plastic table cloths work very well). It is very easy to clean up your mess by carrying the bundle of leftovers to your compost pile. Attach a loop of chenille stem to the back of the wreath for hanging. Chenille stems are soft and will not scratch a wall or door.

The stems of goldenrod are strong and tough and can be easily inserted into a straw base. Or use fern pins as described below.

Trim stems of goldenrod 2 inches beyond flower heads. Hold together three or four heads and attach to straw wreath with fern pin. Place pin over stems of the goldenrod and push into the base at an angle so the ends will not protrude through the back. Begin wreath by filling the inside circle, overlapping the ends of the first cluster with the flowers in the next cluster. Cover the outside circle with clusters as you did the inner circle. Finish by filling in the front of the wreath, all materials facing in the same direction as the inner and outer circles. If you need more material, hang the unfinished wreath in the garage or other dry area out of direct light. Add more goldenrod to fill the base as it becomes available.

Adding accent material to a wreath of this type is easier if the materials are wired to a floral pick first and the ends of the picks inserted through the goldenrod and into the straw base. Pick small clusters of achillea, leaving the terminal shoots to develop into more flowers. Strip the leaves on the stems and wire the clusters to a pick. I insert my picks into a piece of Styrofoam with flower heads down and hang the Styrofoam up. The materials are ready to use in the wreath as soon as they are dry.

Pick heads of Queen-Anne's-Lace just after the flowers open and hang to dry. I have inserted the fresh heads into the wreath, adding a fresh perennial sunflower to the center, and they dried beautifully. The Queen-Anne's-lace made a lacy collar around the sunflower. Try adding all materials to the wreath base fresh; if they do not dry to suit you, remove and add the material you have dried by other methods.

The celosia should be cut and hung to dry before adding to the wreath. Break off small clusters from a large head of crested celosia and add a floral pick to the stem. The bee balm was dried before using as well; some of the flower brackets will remain around the dark center adding color to the wreath. Save the leaves from the bee balm for potpourri, as they are very fragrant.

Decorate the goldenrod base with the red, yellow and white flower clusters in a random design, or try a structured design, grouping the materials together in a pleasing crescent shape around the base of the wreath. Experiment with flowers in your area for a totally different look. Tie a yellow ribbon into a large bow and add to the top of the wreath, hang the wreath, and enjoy.

Summer Flowers in Antique Frame

Large oval frame with convex glass
Fabric of your choice for background
Assortment of silica dried summer flowers
Aleene's Designer Tacky glue

Fig. 2-12 and Color Fig. 7 show placement of foliage and flowers, which include rose buds, ferns, blue salvia, button mums, wild daisies, globe amaranth, blue and white veronica, dahlias, pansies, and button marigolds. First, cover background with fabric: trim fabric to fit cardboard, and glue in place. Position ferns, then glue them in position. Starting at the lower end, place largest flowers, such as dahlias. Check that the glass will not touch them, then glue in place; begin to add medium-sized flowers, then glue to fabric. Fill in design with small flowers to complete.

Place glass frame over design; stand picture up, holding glass in place, and gently tap frame on table to release small pieces of broken materials. Remove glass and brush away particles. Replace glass over the design and add picture frame. Seal the edges on the back of the frame with tape to keep moisture out. Hang picture away from direct, bright light, which will cause flowers to fade.

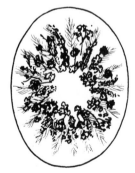

Fig 2-12 Positioning ferns and flowers in an oval frame.

Artemesia, Celosia, and Globe Thistle Bundle

Artemesia, globe thistle, Joe-Pye weed, wild grasses, suveroni, liatris,
    celosia
2 yards wine-colored moire ribbon
Wire

    A large, elegant bundle of summer blooms offers a way of displaying
the beauty of dried materials (Color Fig. 15). Collect and arrange materials all in one color range, or mix complementary colors. The bundle
may be displayed in a large vase or hung on a wall or door. If given to
a friend, include the names of the materials and a few seeds from your
garden so your friend can grow the flowers, too.

    Select long stems of artemesia with well-developed flower heads.
Lay eight to ten stems on a table, in a fan shape (see Color Fig. 15).
Wire the stems together securely. Begin adding the suveroni, Joe-Pye
weed, and other materials to the front of the artemesia. Trim the ends
of all the materials except the artemesia to a length about $\frac{2}{3}$ the distance
from the top of the bundle. Wire small clusters of materials together
and wire to the artemesia at the point where the bow will cover the
ends. Only the ends of the artemesia should extend below the ribbon
bow. Use the largest heads of celosia just above the bow as a focal point
on the bundle.

    Attach a wire loop to the back of the bundle about $\frac{1}{3}$ the distance
from the top. If the wire loop is placed behind the bow, the bundle will
tip forward when hung on a wall. Tie the ribbon into a large bow and
wire to front of bundle.

Hydrangea Wreath with Strawflowers

12-inch Styrofoam wreath
Stardust gyp from Lamrite's
2 large bunches of strawflowers
6 to 8 large heads of hydrangea
2½ yards "Homespun Cluny" ribbon, size 40, color 120, from WFR
    Ribbon Co.
Aleene's Designer Tacky Glue
Wire, florist picks, chenille stem

Hydrangeas are one of the showiest of the summer and early fall flowers and one of the easiest to air dry. They bloom in almost all areas and do well along the seashore and in shady areas where other flowers cannot grow. The range of varieties is large, with flowers in colors of white, pink, and blue. A blue color can be achieved by adding aluminum sulfate to the soil to increase its acidity.

Pick the large flower heads in all stages of maturity and they will retain their color. White flowers begin to blush pink, then deepen to shades of beige when finally dry. The blue shades turn many interesting shades, beginning with the blues and turning to shades of green. Try each shade for your designs. Cut the blossoms, attach the stems to a coat hanger with a rubber band, and hang in a well-ventilated area until dry. The dried blossoms are very fragile and will shatter as they are used, but each large head has so many clusters that you don't need to worry about the loss of a few flowers.

The lovely hydrangea wreath seen in Color Fig. 15 was designed by Elenore Hartman of the Guilford Garden Club in Guilford, CT. Handle the hydrangea carefully to minimize the shattering of the small flowers. Break the large blossoms into small clusters, each cluster having as long a stem as possible. Begin wreath by dipping the stems into the glue and inserting the stems into the Styrofoam base, covering the outside edge first. Place clusters close together, adding as many clusters as needed to hide the base. Add clusters to the inside edge next. Finish with clusters placed on the front of the Styrofoam base. The stems are brittle so handle carefully. Fill in areas with more clusters if needed to hide the base and keep a uniformly rounded shape to the wreath.

Decorate the hydrangea wreath with strawflowers and stardust gyp. Strawflowers are purchased with wires attached; cut wires to desired length and insert through hydrangeas and into Styrofoam base. If you have a supply of strawflowers from your garden, they may be used on this wreath without wiring. Dip the back of the strawflower in glue and gently place the strawflower on the hydrangea base, "nestling" them down into the hydrangeas. Gluing the blossoms isn't as secure as using the wired strawflowers, but it offers a use for flowers that you didn't wire before drying. Strawflowers should be picked when the blossom is fully developed, but before the center petals begin to open. If picked too late the flower will shatter, but save the petals for use as color in potpourri.

Finish decorating the wreath by adding pieces of stardust gyp, breaking the stems into clusters. Dip the stems into the glue and gently place the stems into the Styrofoam base.

Tie the ribbon into a large bow and wire to a florist pick. Insert the florist pick into the Styrofoam base. Cut a 3-inch length of chenille stem and bend into a loop, twisting the ends together. Dip the ends into the glue and insert into the back of the wreath, bending the loop up. Allow glue to dry before hanging the wreath.

Artemesia Heart on Wire Frame

12-inch by 14-inch wire heart frame from K.I.T.I.
$\frac{1}{4}$ lb. green eucalyptus, 4 oz. flocked gyp from Lamrite's
1 dozen white strawflowers, 1 lb. silver king artemesia from THE
    POSIE PATCH
2 yards blue moire ribbon
Florist wire
Glue or glue gun

Fig. 2-14 Wire heart frame covered with artemisia and decorated with strawflowers and ribbon. Designed by Elenore Hartman. See also Color Fig. 13.

Remove the flower head on each stem of artemesia, leaving a length of stem about 4 to 5 inches and set the flowers aside. Bundle together the heavy stems of artemesia and gently curve around the wire heart frame. Start at the top of the heart and wire the bundles tightly to the frame, overlapping the ends as needed. Fill the frame with bundles, making the heart shape about 3 inches wide and 2 inches thick.

Begin adding the reserved flower heads to the front of the heart, starting at the center top. The flower heads should face in the same direction on both sides of the heart. Dip the ends of each flower head in glue or squeeze a little melted glue on each stem, insert the ends into the wired artemesia base, and completely cover the base with the flower heads.

Break off clusters of the preserved gyp, dip the ends into glue or use glue gun, and cover the front of the heart with the gyp. Decorate the top of the heart with the white strawflowers and the eucalyptus as shown in Fig. 2-14, cutting the stems as needed and gluing to the heart.

Tie the ribbon into a large bow and wire to the center of the heart. To hang the heart, add a wire loop to the back behind the ribbon, attaching the loop to the wire frame.

Hydrangea Wreath with Lavender Flowers

12-inch Styrofoam wreath base
Purple globe amaranth, pearly everlasting, lavender & white statice
Suveroni (a heather-like lavender spike flower from Holland,
    purchased from florist or garden center)
6 to 8 heads of dried hydrangea
3 yards lavender moire ribbon
Aleene's Designer Tacky Glue
Chenille stem, wire, florist picks

Referring to Color Fig. 15 and the basic instructions for using hydrangea beginning on page 86, cover the Styrofoam ring with the clusters of dried hydrangea.

Globe amaranth buds must be wired before drying. Cut the wires

89

at different lengths from the flower head, and insert the wire into the foam base. Break the dried materials into small pieces, and wire small clusters to florist picks, inserting picks into the base. Decorate the top and bottom of the wreath, leaving a space at the bottom for a bow.

Cut two 9-inch lengths of ribbon, fold into loops, and wire the loops to a florist pick. Insert ribbon loops into each side of top decoration. Tie remaining ribbon into a bow and wire the bow to a florist pick. Insert the bow at the bottom of wreath in the center of the decorative materials.

Cut a 4-inch length of chenille stem and fold into a loop. Twist the ends of the chenille stem together, dip ends into glue and insert ends into back of wreath. Bend the loop up and allow to dry before hanging wreath.

Straw Heart with Hydrangea and Strawflowers

Straw heart wreath from Lamrite's
Stardust gyp from Lamrite's
1 dozen pink strawflowers, 1 dozen orange globe amaranth from The
    Posie Patch
5 yards white picot ribbon, $\frac{3}{8}$ inch wide
5 yards peach picot ribbon, $\frac{1}{4}$ inch wide
Glue gun, florist picks, chenille stem

This wreath, also designed by Elenore Hartman, can be seen in Color Fig. 13. Refer to basic instructions for using dried hydrangea beginning on page 86. Break the hydrangea into clusters. Using a glue gun, attach small clusters to the straw base, covering the sides and front of the heart. Decorate the wreath with the strawflowers, cutting the wires and inserting them into the straw base. Add the globe amaranth, pushing the wires into the straw base. Break the gyp into small clusters and wire to a florist pick, pushing picks into base.

Cut white and peach ribbons into 6-inch lengths, fold ribbons into two loops, and wire both sets of loops to the same florist pick. Add loops of ribbon next to each strawflower as shown. Fold remaining ribbon into large loops, about 6 inches long, and wire loops together in a cluster. Attach ribbon cluster to point of heart wreath under the flowers, using the glue gun or florist pick.

Cut a 4 inch length of chenille stem and fold into a loop. Attach loop to back of wreath with a fern pin or push end of loop into straw base and glue to secure.

Hydrangea and Ribbon Wreath

14-inch brass ring from K.I.T.I.
1 dozen orange globe amaranth from The Posie Patch
5 yards peach picot ribbon, $\frac{1}{4}$ inch wide
3 to 4 large dried hydrangea flowers
Stardust gyp from Lamrite's
Light brown or beige florist tape

Lots of ribbons and hydrangea make a very gay wreath, as seen in Color Fig. 13. Begin by covering the wire ring with the florist tape, stretching the tape as you wind it around the wire. The florist tape will stick to itself as it is stretched and gives a firm base for attaching the flower clusters. The surface of the tape is semi-tacky and prevents slippage of the flower clusters.

Break the hydrangea and gyp into small pieces approximately 3 inches long. Cut the wires of the globe amaranth to a length of 2 inches. Begin to make small clusters of the dried materials, holding together two or three pieces of gyp, one cluster of hydrangea, and one globe amaranth. Twist florist tape around the ends of the cluster. Continue to make clusters, making enough to fill the ring before attaching to ring.

Place one cluster on the taped ring and secure with small piece of florist tape. The tape may be left in a long length and each cluster added one after the other. Cut ribbon into 9-inch lengths and fold into loops. Add a cluster of ribbon loops at the end of each flower cluster, securing the ribbon to the ring with tape. Add the next cluster of flowers, covering the ends of the previous cluster, filling the ring completely.

Lavender Potpourri Baskets

27 or 29 stems of fresh lavender
4 yards picot satin ribbon, ⅜ inch wide
Long needle or heavy wire
Styrofoam base
String, scissors

Fresh lavender blossoms and ribbon can be woven into small pot-pourri baskets, to be filled with dried lavender and rose buds for a closet sachet. Pick the longest and heaviest stems of lavender just before the blossoms begin to open on the stem. Pick the lavender after the dew has dried in early morning, and before the sun shines on the flowers. The sun will dissipate the perfume in the flowers. (Flower stems that have grown too fast and have opened their little flowers may be used for this project, because you will add dried lavender to the basket to provide the heavy perfume scent that may have been lost in the older flowers.)

Refer to Figs. 2-15 through 2-18 and assemble the materials needed for a basket. I pick only enough lavender to make one basket at a time. The flower stems dry out very fast and become brittle, so they must be used very soon after picking.

Hold a cluster of blossoms together at the base of the flower heads, tie securely with a string (Fig. 2-16). Gently bend each flower stem down over the flower cluster as shown in Fig. 2-17. Support the flower cluster on a long needle or piece of heavy wire stuck in a piece of Styrofoam. Slip the end of the ribbon under one stem and push the ribbon into the flower cluster. Carefully lift the stems and weave the ribbon in and out around the base of the cluster. Weave three or four rows of ribbon making a flat bottom for the basket. Remove the basket and turn it right side up on the pin (Fig. 2-18). Continue weaving the ribbon around the sides of the basket, keeping the ribbon close together and making the sides of the basket straight.

To make the top edge, fold one stem over to the inside of the basket, with the fold ½ inch above the last row of ribbon. Weave the ribbon between the folded stem and pull down tight to make a point (see Fig. 2-15). Fold the next stem to the inside of the basket over the ribbon and even with the top of the basket. Weave the end of each of these stems in and out of the ribbon rows inside the basket to secure the

Fig. 2-15 Fresh lavender stems woven with ribbon into a potpourri basket, filled with dried lavender and rose buds.

Fig. 2-16 Materials needed for lavender basket.

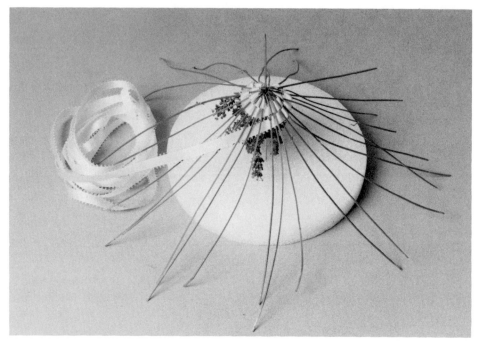

Fig. 2-17 Base of basket woven with ribbon

Fig. 2-18 Basket sides and pointed top edge

stems. Trim off the excess length of stem. Continue to bend each stem to the inside of the basket, making a point and securing the ribbon between the stems. Tie remaining ribbon into two small bows. Attach a loop of ribbon on each side of the basket with glue and cover ends of loop with a bow.

Allow the basket to dry, filling with tissue paper to support the sides of the basket. When the basket is dry, fill with dried lavender flowers and top the basket with small dried rose buds. The basket may be hung in a closet or used as a Christmas ornament, scenting the tree with lavender. Add lavender oil to basket as needed to increase the lavender perfume.

Fig. 2-19 Lavender bundles, fresh lavender stems woven with ribbon to enclose flower heads. Refer to lavender basket for basic instructions.

Victorian Lavender Bottles

Dried lavender was used by Victorian ladies as a perfume scent for sachets for their dresser drawers and closets. The most unusual and dainty sachets were called "bottles" and made from the fresh stems of lavender and ribbon (see Fig. 2-19). The technique for making the small "bottles" is similar to the lavender baskets.

Cut 23 to 25 stems of fresh lavender. Tie the flowers tightly together at the base of the heads. Gently bend each stem over the flower cluster and hold together at the bottom. Cut a $1\frac{1}{2}$ yard length of narrow ribbon and insert the end into the base of the flower cluster. Weave the ribbon over and under each of the stems, pushing the ribbon close to the base. Continue weaving the ribbon down over the flower cluster. Tie the ribbon around the stems at the base of the cluster. Fold an 18 inch length of ribbon into a bow and tie to the stems. Add lavender oil to bundles to revive the perfume.

Porthole Window Display

The arrangement pictured in Color Fig. 14 was my entry in a 1985 Standard Flower Show presented by Leete's Island Garden Club. The arrangement won a Second Place ribbon in a class calling for all dried material, and the round porthole window was definitely a challenge. I tried to echo the feeling of movement and curves within the window without blocking the view through the window. The colors in the abalone shell and protea matched the colors in the draperies on the window. Select similar dried materials and enjoy trying something different with your arranging.

1 large and 3 medium protea blossoms
4 strelitzia leaves, sprayed with white paint
1 large abalone or other shell
1 piece of sand shale, driftwood, or a flat rock
2 to 3 sprays wild sea grass
Large oval pin holder
Florist clay

Cut a small piece of florist clay and attach the pin holder near the back of the base to leave space for the large shell. (Florist clay is stiff and hard, but it can be softend by squeezing it in your hands.)

Select tall, curved leaves, trim the long stems to the height desired, and push the stems into the pin holder. To make a stem turn out to the side, cut the base at an angle across the stem. Cut the heavy stems of the protea blossoms to the desired height and push the stems into the pin holder. Soften a small piece of floral clay and attach the large shell to the base in front of the pin holder, covering the pin holder and stems. Add small bunches of dried grasses to the sides, placing the stems in the pin holder behind the abalone shell.

Corn Husk Wreath

14-inch Styrofoam wreath
Dried corn husks, purchased or collected
Fern pins, florist picks, medium florist wire
4 yards Cascade ribbon, size 40, color 332 from WFR Ribbon Co.
5 large blue corn husk flowers
Red plume celosia
Stardust gyp from Lamrite's
Chenille stem

The cornhusk wreath shown in Color Fig. 5 will provide a very stylish welcome on any door.

Preparing Corn Husks. Remove corn husks from ear of corn, removing one husk at a time so as to minimize splitting. (Save all split husks and shreds and dry for use in other projects.) Corn may be cooked in the microwave oven before husking, follow cooking directions in your cook book. Corn cooked in the microwave is tasty and easy, the bonus being corn husks that are pliable for up to 2 days and ready to use.

Lay corn husks on a flat surface covered with newspaper and place in a dry area with good air circulation. Do not crowd the corn husks because they will mildew easily. If some corn husks mildew, try soaking in warm water and a small amount of household bleach. This may remove the mildew, if not discard the corn husks and collect more. The corn husks will curl as they dry, but they will flatten out when soaked in warm water again and folded into loops. Collect a large supply during the summer and store in brown paper bags until ready to use. Do not use plastic bags as moisture may collect and cause the corn husks to mildew.

Covering the Wreath. Separate the widest husks and lay aside to be made into loops for decorating the wreath. Soak the narrower husks in a large container of hot water, adding a small amount of glycerine to help soften the husks. Leave husks in the water and remove one or two at a time and begin wrapping the Styrofoam base. Pin the ends on one of the flat sides, pushing the fern pins in at an angle so the ends do not protrude through the back. Overlap the edges of the corn husks, being sure to cover the foam base completely. The husks will shrink as they dry and expose the foam base if not overlapped. Hang up the covered base in a dry area with good air circulation until completely dry. Do not lay the wreath down since the back of the wreath may mildew.

Remove from the water any remaining corn husk strips and lay out to dry again; do not discard, but save for other projects. (You may also gradually cover the base with husks, adding to it as the husks are collected after each meal!)

Begin making loops from the wide strips of corn husks. Place husks in hot water, adding glycerine to the water to soften the strips. Remove a husk from the water and open it out flat, smoothing with your fingers. Fold the husk in half and hold the ends together, trimming the ends if necessary. Gather the ends of the loop together and wire the ends with florist wire, leaving a half inch length of wire extending beyond end of the loop. The loop may be added to the covered base at this time by pushing the wire into the foam base, or a number of loops may be made and set aside before decorating the base.

Another method of making and adding loops is to use a fern pin to pin each individual loop to the base without wiring the ends of the loop. I like the wiring method because it is easier to control the ends of the loops.

Refer to Color Fig. 5 and Fig. 2-20 for ideas for placing the loops, choosing a style suitable to the design you are planning.

Decorating the Wreath. Refer to instructions in Part One for making corn husk flowers and make five large flowers in colors that com-

Fig. 2-20 Two ideas for placement of corn husk loops on wreath.

plement the setting and the ribbon you have chosen. If you choose colors other than the red and blue used here, select celosia in any of the other colors available to suit your design.

Pin the large corn husk flowers to the wreath base using fern pins. Add stems of celosia and gyp between the flowers and at the ends of the design. Cut 2 yards of ribbon, tie into a large bow, and wire the bow to the top of the wreath. Cut remaining ribbon into 4-inch lengths and fold into loops. Wire loops to a florist pick and place loops in and around flowers, pushing florist pick into foam base. Fold a chenille stem into a loop and add to the back of the wreath for hanging.

Corn Husk Fringe on Wire Frame

6-inch crimped wire ring
Corn husk strips
4 sprays glycerine-treated leaves
5 large corn husk flowers
Wire

A charming decorative wreath (Color Fig. 8) can be made from leftover pieces of corn husks that are too narrow for flowers or loops. I find it easiest to add the strips to the wire frame as I collect them while they are green and pliable. The husks will turn white as they dry. If dry strips are used to make the wreath, soak the corn husks in hot water, adding a small amount of glycerine to soften the husks.

Select two or three narrow strips of equal length. Hold them together and fold strips in half. Place folded end to the inside of the wire ring. Open the folded end and bring the ends through the loop over the wire, pulling ends tight. Continue adding strips around the ring, pushing the strips as close together as possible. The corn husks will shrink as they dry; if there are open spaces later, just add a few more corn husks. Shred the corn husk strips by pulling the husks apart with your fingers or a heavy needle. As the strips dry, some will curl and add fullness to the wreath. Trim any ends that are uneven. Hang the wreath in a dry area. If any of the corn husks remain dark after drying, cut away and add fresh husks.

Refer to the directions in Part One for making corn husk flowers. Make five flowers in the colors of your choice and wire the flowers to the corn husk ring. Add glycerine foliage at the end of the flower cluster. Sumac was used in this design. Add a loop of wire to the top of the wreath for hanging.

Corn Stalks and Dried Weeds Arrangement

3 to 5 dried corn stalks with tassels attached
2 to 3 corn husk flowers
Mullein, goldenrod, wild grasses
Crock or other large container
Large pin holder or large block of Oasis

Corn stalks and other dried material can make a striking arrangement for the corner of any room, as seen in Color Fig. 9. Pick and dry grasses, goldenrod, and mullein seed heads, cutting each stem at least double the height of your container. Cut tall stalks from a corn patch or purchase from a garden center or roadside vegetable stand. If stalks are still green, allow them to dry in a well-ventilated area to prevent mildew. They may be hung upside down or right side up, allowing the leaves and tassels to droop and curve as they dry, or the leaves may be shaped into curves and held together with hair clips or paper clips until dry.

To make corn husk flowers with corn cobs attached, first select ears of corn with a portion of the stem still attached and carefully pull back the corn husks, leaving them attached at the base of the corn cob. Break off the corn cob leaving a 1-inch piece of corn. Curl the corn husks and hold in place until dry with hair clips or paper clips. Hang the corn cobs to dry in a well-ventilated area to prevent mildew. The corn cob when dry gives the appearance of a flower center. Wire ends to a heavy stem for adding to the arrangement.

Place pin holder or Oasis in bottom of container. Place the tallest cornstalks into the container, pushing the stems down into the pin holder or Oasis. Develop the design using the tallest corn stalk as the center focal point. Add a corn stalk to either side, cutting the stalks 2 to 3 inches shorter. Continue adding corn stalks and other dried materials to the front of the design, cutting the stems as needed to fill the container. Place 2 to 3 large corn husk flowers in the front of the design. Arrangements of this type are appropriate for either outdoors or indoors. The materials are heavy enough not to be damaged by wind and rain.

Echoes of Fall

Wreath of Dried Dock

14-inch straw wreath from Lamrite's
5 oz. bundle of orange gypsy grass from Lamrite's
Wild grass heads, picked after fully dried
Wild dock seed heads, picked in early stages of color change
Wire, florist picks
3 yards Super Beau Vel, size 9, color 245 (burnt orange) from WFR
  Ribbon Co.

Wild dock grows in abundance along roadsides and in fields and is ready to pick as soon as the seed heads have developed. The dock will dry and retain the color it is when picked. In early summer the dock will be a light green and begins to turn to shades of peach/beige as the season progresses. Mid-fall colors range from light to medium brown and by late fall reaches a deep mahagony. Each color is suitable for fall wreaths and arrangements, as in Color Fig. 2. Picking the dock in the early stages reduces the amount of shattering and loss of seeds. This is definitely a messy dried material and should be handled as little as possible if used in the house. Spraying a wreath or arrangement with plastic coating spray helps to seal the seed heads and cut down on some of the shattering.

The dock may be picked and dried before using in a wreath, but I like to make my wreath as I collect the dock. Cut the stems about 5 to 6 inches long and insert the heavy stems directly into a straw wreath. Begin placing the dock seed heads at the center bottom of the wreath, filling in the inner circle and along the outside circle. Add materials from center bottom to center top on each side of wreath, leaving an opening at the top for a bow. Fill the center of the wreath with dock.

Break stems of the dried grass heads into various lengths and wire to a florist pick. Push the picks into the straw base, adding clusters of grass throughout the wreath. Break off clusters of gypsy grass and push the stems directly into the straw wreath or wire them to a florist pick and add to the wreath.

Tie the orange ribbon into a large bow and wire to top of wreath. Add a loop of wire on the back for hanging the wreath.

Grapevine Wreath with Citrus Flowers

16-inch grapevine wreath
3 grapefruit flowers, 3 orange flowers, and 2 grapefruit roses
Small pine cones and dried seed pods
1 gold corn husk flower
Clusters of dried tansy, dried seed heads from Clematis
4 yards gold craft velvet ribbon
Glue gun, scissors, pins, wire

Dried materials may be wired to the grapevine wreath but using a glue gun is preferable. Attach one end of the ribbon to the top of the grapevine wreath on the back using the glue gun. Wind the ribbon around the wreath, gluing the end on the back, overlapping the ends. Tie the remaining ribbon into a large bow and set aside.

Using Color Fig. 3 as a guide, glue the seed pods, pine cones, and dried flowers to the grapevine wreath. Choose the largest materials and place them in a cluster at the center bottom of the wreath. Add pods and flowers along each side of the wreath, leaving a space open at the top for the bow. Spray the wreath with plastic coating to add sheen to the materials and improve the colors in the pods and flowers.

Make one medium-sized corn husk flower, following the directions in Part One and using a deep gold dye. Add the flower to the wreath after the wreath has been sprayed with plastic coating.

To make a grapefruit or orange flower, cut the fruit in half and remove the fruit as sections or juice. Scrape the shell with a spoon to remove all the membrane, making the shell as thin as possible. Cut the shell with scissors into narrow strips, leaving a center section about 1 inch across. Insert a piece of wire up and back down through the center, twisting the ends of the wire together (Fig. 2-21). Trim the ends of each section of shell into a point, curl the strips to the center, and pin the strips together to hold them in place. Hang the "flower" upside down until dry, and then remove the pins.

Fig. 2-21 How to cut an orange flower, wiring the bottom before drying.

To make a grapefruit rose, remove fruit and membrane from a cut grapefruit, making the shell as thin as possible. Cut one slit in skin from edge to center of shell (Fig. 2-22). Turn shell inside out, rolling the skin over as shown in the diagram. Roll one side of the slit into the center and use a pin to hold it in place. Pin outside edges holding the shell together in the shape of a rose. Allow to dry completely before removing the pins.

Attach the citrus flowers to the grapevine wreath using the glue gun. "Roses" may also be made from oranges, lemons, or limes. Fruit that has become too dry for eating are excellent for this project.

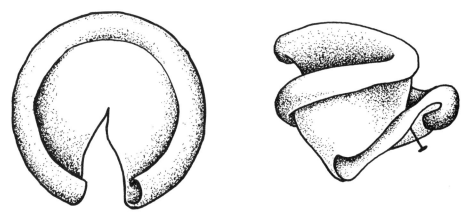

Fig. 2-22 Cutting and pinning a grapefruit peel to make a citrus rose.

Twig Basket with Corn Husk Flowers and Bittersweet

10-inch diameter twig basket with handle from Lamrite's
5 large gold corn husk flowers
1 large spray of bittersweet, 36 to 40 inches
4 clusters glycerine-treated leaves
1 small artificial bird
2 8-inch blocks Sahara II Dry Floral Foam
1 sheet Oasis Moss Mate
Floral pins, wire

Place one block Dry Floral Foam in center of basket; cut second block in pieces and wedge into basket tightly, filling basket completely with foam. Push floral pins through bottom of basket into foam to secure foam to basket. Foam may be glued to bottom of basket if the arrangement is to be permanent. Cover top of foam with Moss Mate.

Pick and use bittersweet when the yellow pods are tightly closed; they will open as they dry, revealing the bright red berries. There will be little or no loss of berries if arranged while the vines are fresh and green.

Using Fig. 2-23 as a guide, place one end of the bittersweet branch in the center of the basket, pushing the end all the way to the bottom of the basket. Extend the branch above the handle and wire the branch to the handle securely. Twist and shape branch into a curve. Twist the end of the branch back over the top of the handle, extending the end down over the edge to the front of the basket. Wire the branch to the front edge of the basket to hold the branch in place. Wire small pieces of bittersweet to the main branch if needed to cover any bare spots and add color to the design. Cover handle with small pieces of bittersweet, wiring in place.

Make five large gold corn husk flowers, following directions in Part One. Arrange three flowers in the front of the basket, following the line of the bittersweet branch. Trim ends of flowers as needed to achieve a pleasing arrangement. Place two flowers in the back of the basket. Add small clusters of bittersweet, the artificial bird, and glycerine-treated foliage to fill in the arrangement.

Fig. 2-23 Twig basket arrangement featuring bittersweet and corn husk sunflowers.

Grapevine Wreath with Cattails

16-inch grapevine wreath
4 yards brown velvet ribbon
4 slim cattails
Dried dock, iris seed pods, dried seed heads of wild grasses
Wire, glue gun
Brown chenille stem

A natural beauty is achieved in this wreath designed by Jacqueline Plant by using only shades of beige and brown. The dock is picked just as it has turned a soft brown. The wild grasses are picked after the heads have opened completely and become fluffy. The cattails have to have been picked in early June and dried. If picked too late in the summer, the cattail heads will burst. Pick various seed heads in shades of beige and brown.

Wrap ribbon around grapevine wreath, gluing ends on back of wreath. Cut a 3-inch length of chenille stem and twist into back of wreath for a hanging loop. Wire cattails together and wire to front of wreath. Glue clusters of dock and iris seed pods to each side of the cattails. Add various lengths of dried grasses to center of wreath, gluing the stems to the cattails. Glue a purchased Canadian goose to wreath, covering the stems. Tie remaining ribbon into a bow and glue to base of wreath.

Fig. 2-24 *Twig wreath with cattails, dried grasses, and Canadian goose, designed by Jacqueline Plant.*

Cornucopia with Chinese Lanterns and Bittersweet

Small wicker cornucopia
4-inch block Sahara II Dry Floral Foam and Oasis Moss Mate from
Lamrite's
10 to 12 stems brown eucalyptus
3 to 4 stems bittersweet, 3 to 4 stems pussy willow, 2 to 3 stems
Chinese lanterns
Goldenrod
Floral pins, glue gun

Fig. 2-25 Cornucopia featuring eucalyptus, bittersweet, and Chinese lanterns.

Place Floral Foam in opening of cornucopia and trim to fit. Cover the foam with the Moss Mate, and hold in place with floral pins. Arrange materials, beginning with stems of eucalyptus, placing longest stems first and filling in with shorter stems as needed. Cut bittersweet into various lengths and push into foam. Cut stems of Chinese lanterns and add to center of design. If lanterns break off of the stem, reattach with glue gun. Add stems of pussy willow and goldenrod to fill out the design. If design becomes tipsy and will not sit flat, carefully remove the arrangement and fill back of cornucopia with stones. Push arrangement back into the opening.

Fall Floral Candle Ring

Tall compote or other container
Styrofoam ring to fit container
Flocked gyp from Lamrite's
White yarrow, gold yarrow, Pearl achillea, white statice, orange straw
    flowers
Florist picks, glue, candle

Any combination of white and yellow materials may be used to make this centerpiece (shown in Color Fig. 8). Other colored material can be added to complement your table decor. I add bright reds, blues, greens or other colors as I change the colors on my table.

Collect the materials listed during the summer and hang to dry. Break off the stems from the white yarrow leaving a 2-inch length of stem. Dip ends into glue and insert into Styrofoam ring, completely covering the outside edge of the ring. Fill in top of ring with gold yarrow, small bunches of Pearl achillea that have been wired to a florist pick, and any other suitable white dried materials. The stems of white statice may be dipped in glue and inserted into the ring. Wire small bunches of flocked gyp to a florist pick and add to ring. Cut wires on strawflowers leaving a 2 inch length, dip wire into glue and insert into ring.

Autumn Arrangement

1 lb. of brown eucalyptus
1 pint "ready-to-use" glycerine from Activa Products, Inc.
20 to 25 stems of gold yarrow
Goldenrod, sweet fern, and rhododendron leaves treated with
    glycerine
Container

This impressive arrangement of soft foliage is shown in Color Fig. 8. Pick golden yarrow when flowers first open and are at their brightest; hang in loose bunches to dry. Lengthen stems for arrangement if needed by attaching a longer natural stem. Preserve goldenrod, sweet fern, and rhododendron leaves with glycerine, as described in Part One. Sweet fern has a wonderful scent that remains after treating with glycerine. The leaves turn a deep, warm brown, much the same color as the rhododendron leaves. The deep scent of preserved eucalyptus and sweet fern in this arrangement is delightful in any room.

As this is a large arrangement, it may be necessary to weight the bottom of your container with stones or sand to prevent it from tipping over. The stems in a large mass arrangement will usually support each other so that it isn't necessary to use floral foam in the container. However, if a wide-mouthed container is used, floral foam may be necessary to support the arrangement.

Begin the design by placing eucalyptus in the container with the longest stems to the back and center of the design. Create a rounded, fan shape with the eucalyptus branches, trimming the ends as necessary. Add longest stems of preserved goldenrod and gold yarrow to the design, and work toward the front, filling in with eucalyptus, goldenrod, and yarrow, trimming stems are needed. Wire or tape stems of sweet fern to wire or other natural stems to lengthen and add to arrangement as filler. Place sweet fern to sides and front, allowing leaves to drape over front edge of container. Fill container completely with as much material as needed to make a large bouquet. Position one large cluster of rhododendron leaves as a focal point at front of container.

Display the arrangement in a warm area if possible to release the aroma of the preserved materials. Mine is in the entry hall, and when the sun shines on it the hall is scented. The gold yarrow will fade in time in the sun, but it can be replaced with fresh material or spray painted.

To store materials when you change the display, pack away in a large box and store in a dry area. The treated materials will last forever and retain their shape and color.

Fall Foliage on Excelsior Wreath

17-inch excelsior wreath from Lamrite's
4 yards "Dover Cluny" ribbon, color 627, size 40 from WFR Ribbon Co.
1 pint "ready-to-use" glycerine from Activa Products, Inc.
6 pieces brown eucalyptus
2 small dried strawberry corn with husks
1 small dried gourd
Sumac foliage, goldenrod, rhododendron leaves
Seed heads from bee balm
Wire, glue gun, fern pins

Collect listed materials and preserve with glycerine following instructions in Part One.

Attach ribbon to back of wreath with a fern pin and wind ribbon around wreath, leaving spaces on the excelsior wreath as shown in Color Fig. 10. Secure end of ribbon on back of wreath, overlapping ends. Tie remaining ribbon into a bow and set aside.

The grouping of materials is started by wiring a bouquet together and then attaching it to the wreath. Begin the bouquet using long pieces of eucalyptus, adding goldenrod and long stems of bee balm. Wire stems together at the point where the stems will be attached to the wreath. Add sumac foliage to the sides of the arrangement. Wire or glue the bouquet to the wreath, extending the ends across the wreath at an angle. Glue bow to the front of the wreath over the dried stems. Add the strawberry corn, small gourd and rhododendron on the right side of the bow, securing to the wreath with a glue gun.

Winter Wonders

Pine Cone Star

15-inch wire star frame from K.I.T.I.
18-inch by 36-inch brown felt or other heavy brown fabric
Pine cones; pinyon, Norway spruce, white spruce
Walnuts, pecans, filberts, almonds
Aleene's Designer Tacky Glue
Glue gun
Spray lacquer
Chenille stem

Cut the brown fabric in half to get two pieces 18 inches square. Place wire star frame on one piece of fabric. Trim around star shape, allowing a 1-inch border beyond the frame. Clip into the sides of the frame and wrap the fabric over each point of the star. Glue the fabric around the wire, stretching the fabric tight on the frame.

Select small, flat pine cones of equal size and glue a row of pine cones to the outside edge of the star. Continue adding various types of cones to the center of the star, gluing each pine cone securely to the fabric. Decorate top of star with small pine cones and nuts. Spray star with clear plastic lacquer to seal the pine cones and add luster to the star.

Cut the reserved piece of fabric to fit the back of the star and glue to back covering the edges of the wire frame. If felt is used, cut the edges the same size as the star. If woven fabric is used, add $\frac{1}{2}$ inch of fabric and turn under the edges before gluing to the back of the star. Glue a chenille loop to the back at the end of one point.

Fig. 2-26 *Pine cones and nuts on a wire star frame.*

Cheese Box with Pine Cones

Wedge-wood cheese box from Bentwood, Inc.
Brown spray paint or wood stain
Pine cones; pinyon, Norway spruce, white spruce, etc.
Various seeds and nuts
Glue gun

Spray top and sides of cheese box with brown paint or dark wood stain. Allow to dry. Glue eight large Norway spruce pine cones around the outside edge of the box lid. Fill in the center of the lid with smaller pine cones and nuts. Add one large decorative seed pod at the top of the lid as shown in Fig. 2-27. Fill box with a supply of pine cone fire starters to give as a housewarming gift.

Pine Cone Fire Starters

Select medium-sized pine cones of any type. Melt old candle wax in a can over hot water. Place pine cone in a small aluminum pie pan and pour the melted wax around the base of the pine cone. Allow wax to cool until almost set. Cut a birthday candle in half and push into the soft wax at the base of the pine cone. Allow wax to harden and remove from the pie pan. Set one or two fire starters in the fireplace and light the small candle. The pine cone and wax will burn, igniting the fire wood.

Pine Cone and Seed Tree

22- to 25-inch wicker tree
Small pine cones, nuts, and seed pods
Sheet moss or Moss Mate
Wire
Small needlenose pliers
Glue gun
Clear plastic spray

Select various types of pine cones, dividing them into different sizes. Beginning with the smallest, begin wiring a row of cones to the

Fig. 2-27 Clockwise from left: Cheese box decorated with pine cones and seed pods. Wicker "tree" covered with pine cones, nuts, and seed pods. Pine cone fire starters.

top of the tree as far up inside as you can reach. It may be necessary to glue the last row or two on the top if the wicker is too narrow. Wire two rows of each type of pod or cone to the tree. Cut Moss Mate or sheet moss in 1-inch strips and glue to the wicker between each row of cones. Alternate colors and textures of pods and cones in each row to add interest to the finished design. Add a large decorative seed pod to the top. Spray tree with clear plastic to add a glossy finish.

Ivy Topiary Tree

3 or 4 small ivy plants or well-rooted ivy cuttings
9-inch green plastic flower pot with drain dish
Chicken wire 18 inches by 27 inches
Potting soil
Wood or metal dowel
Wire

The ivy tree pictured in Fig. 2-28 is supported by a tall spiral shaped tree made from brass. It was found at a garage sale and may be available from a florist or garden center. If not, make a tree shape by rolling the chicken wire into a cone; wire together along the seam using medium-weight wire. Trim away excess wire to make the bottom edge even with the top of the flower pot. Set tree shape aside.

Fill flower pot with potting soil. Moisten soil with water and let pot stand for a while allowing soil to settle. Add soil if necessary to fill pot. Remove small ivy plants from the pots and trim away excess roots and shake off excess soil. Space ivy plants evenly around inside edge of pot. Do not crowd plants or the ivy will become root bound very soon. Water plants to settle the soil and allow to sit for a short time. Add potting soil if necessary to fill pot (soil should be 1 inch below top edge of pot).

Insert wood or wire dowel in center of pot, pushing the dowel all the way to the bottom of the pot. Place wire cone over end of the dowel and wire top of cone to the dowel. Shape bottom edge of cone to fit inside of pot with edge of wire sitting on the surface of the soil. Carefully pull the stems of ivy to the outside of the chicken wire and weave stems in and out through the openings in the wire.

Water once a week and fertilize ivy plants once a month. Place tree in window with strong light and some sun during winter months to encourage continuous growth. Turn pot each week to encourage ivy to grow evenly around pot. As ends of ivy lengthen, weave the ends into the wire, filling cone shape. The Ivy tree pictured was planted early in April and by Christmas the tree was covered but not as full as it should be. Another six months to a year should produce a full tree. During the summer months, place the tree outside under a tree but don't forget to water if there is insufficient rain.

Fig. 2-28 Ivy topiary and growing wreath. Clockwise from left: ivy topiary tree; living ivy wreath; heart topiary; topiary ball.

To start the tree from ivy cuttings, space five or six cuttings around top of pot. Allow cuttings to grow until they are well rooted. Trim ends of ivy to encourage branching and increase the number of stems to add fullness to the tree. Using cuttings will take longer to fill the tree shape than if small plants are used.

Ivy Topiary Ball

Wire topiary ball from Topiary, Inc.
Ivy cuttings
Sphagnum moss
Hormex rooting compound
Nylon fishing line
Fern pins
3 yards red satin picot ribbon, $\frac{1}{4}$ inch wide

Place sphagnum moss in a large bucket and add warm water; allow the moss to become completely saturated. Remove large handfuls of the moss from the water and squeeze out excess water. Begin filling the center of the wire ball frame with the wet moss, extending the moss beyond the wire frame and packing tightly. The moss will shrink as it settles and dries, so it is important that the frame is as full as possible to insure enough moss for the ivy roots to grow.

Tie the nylon fishing line to the wire frame and wrap the fishing line around the ball, overlapping the line and leaving 1-inch spaces of moss exposed. The fishing line gives extra support to the moss and prevents sagging, maintaining the ball shape after the ivy is planted.

Use a knife or other narrow tool to make small holes in the moss in the open spaces between the pieces of fishing line. Gently insert rooted cuttings of ivy and press the moss around the roots. If cuttings do not have roots, dip cut ends into rooting compound and insert deep into the moss.

Maintain even moistness in the sphagnum moss until cuttings have rooted and started to grow. A large plastic bag may be placed around the ball and tied at the bottom to help hold in moisture until the cuttings have rooted.

Water once a week by running water over the ball, holding it over the sink and allowing the excess water to drain away. Fertilize once a month. During the dry winter months spray the ivy with a plant mister between watering. Place the ivy ball in a bright, sunny window when new growth has started, but check often for dryness. Rotate ball each week to encourage growth evenly around ball. Pin the new growth to the ball with fern pins, inserting the small hair roots into the moss so they can root and start to grow, covering the ball with new plants. Place the ivy ball outside under a tree during the summer, but do not forget to water if there is insufficient rain.

The ivy ball pictured was planted in early May with cuttings, and by Christmas the moss was completely covered with ivy. Decorate the ivy ball with small bunches of artificial berries and bows. (Check the artificial materials to be sure the colors do not run when water is added.) Wind the metal dowel with the red ribbon, gluing the ends of the ribbon to the top and bottom of the dowel. Fold remaining ribbon into long loops as pictured and pin to bottom of ball with fern pins.

Ivy Heart Topiary

6-inch pot of ivy or 3 to 4 rooted ivy cuttings
Heart-shaped topiary frame, or coat hanger
Florist ties

The ivy heart pictured in Fig. 2-28 was started from a well-established plant of ivy in a 6-inch pot. A heart-shaped wire frame was placed in the center of the pot and the ivy stems were tied to the frame with green florist ties. As the plant increased in size the stems were woven in and out to fill the shape.

A wire coat hanger can be used to create various shapes such as a circle, star or tree. Bend the coat hanger to desired shape and straighten the curved end to insert into the pot. Paint the end of the wire to prevent rust, as in time the wire may deteriorate and break off in the pot. Push the wire into the center of the plant and wind ivy around the wire.

Living Ivy Wreath

Ivy or other types of vine cuttings (variegated euonymus)
16-inch double box wire wreath
Hormex rooting powder
Green plastic trash bag cut into 3-inch-wide strips
Fern pins
Scissors

Place sphagnum moss in large container and add warm water, allowing moss to become completely saturated. Remove large handfuls of moss from the container and squeeze out excess water. Place moss inside the wire frame, packing the moss tightly and extending the moss above the top edge at least 1 inch.

Pin end of one plastic strip to moss wreath and wind the strip around wreath, overlapping edges $\frac{1}{2}$ inch. Add strips of plastic as needed, overlapping ends and covering wreath completely. Cut small slits in top and sides of plastic with scissors or a sharp knife. Dip plant cuttings into water and then into the rooting powder. Insert cuttings into openings in plastic, pushing ends well into center of the moss wreath. Press moss around ends of cuttings and pin cuttings to wreath with fern pins. Cover top and sides of wreath with cuttings.

Place wreath on large plastic tray (I use a plastic turntable generally used in kitchen cupboards to hold spices). The tray protects table surfaces from dampness and holds moisture around the wreath when water is added. Water as often as needed to maintain even moistness of moss until cuttings are rooted and wreath shows new growth on ends of cuttings. Water once a week after cuttings are established and fertilize once a month. Place wreath in sunny window during the winter, turning the wreath each week to insure continuous growth on all sides of the wreath.

Euonymus and ivy wreaths were planted at the same time in early April. Euonymus is slow growing and takes longer to cover the wreath shape. The euonymus wreath may be brought in the house during the winter or left outside in a protected spot as it is winter hardy. (The cuttings I used came from my flower bed so I set my wreath in the flower bed protecting the wreath with the parent plant.)

Place ivy wreath outside under a tree during the summer and be

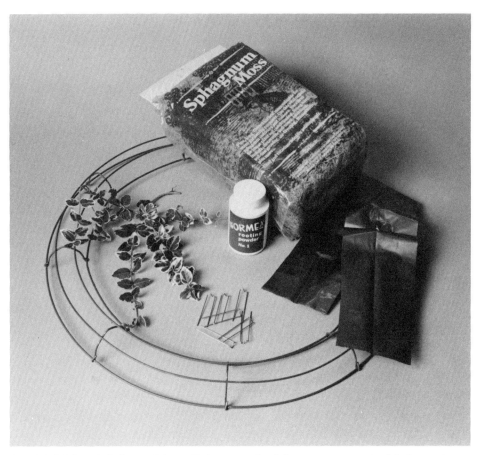

Fig. 2-29 Materials for making a living wreath: Sphagnum moss, double-box wire frame, rooting powder, fern pins, plastic strips, plant cuttings.

sure to water if there is insufficient rain. Clean tray and inspect wreath for small bugs and spiders before bringing into the house for the winter.

A number of different plants can be used in growing wreaths. Try using various ground covers such as sweet woodruff. This lacy-leafed perennial has a lovely scent and pretty white flowers in May. The leaves are used for making May wine. Pinch back ends to encourage growth, and dry the cuttings for potpourri. Compact growing herbs are excellent choices for living wreaths and you will have a constant supply of fresh

Fig. 2-30 Making a living wreath.

herbs during the winter. Pinching off pieces of the herbs for use in the kitchen encourages lush growth, and the wreath will fill out very quickly. A living herb wreath would make a wonderful gift for that special friend who loves gardening and cooking. Remember to include the names of the herbs and the care instructions with the wreath.

Growing wreaths may be hung on a wall and decorated with other natural materials and ribbons for the holidays. Soak the wreath in water to insure sufficient moisture for the plants. Allow the wreath to stand so that any excess moisture will have drained away before hanging on the wall. Wipe the back of the wreath to remove any dirt that might soil the walls. Take the wreath down once a week and water. Remove decorations if necessary to prevent damaging the decorations.

Fig. 2-31 Living wreath partially covered with plants.

Christmas Wreath with Yellow Roses

16-inch double box wire wreath
1 yard dark green fabric
Natural evergreens, glycerine-preserved andromeda
10 yellow rose buds preserved in silica gel
10 large ivy leaves preserved in glycerine
10 small plumes red celosia
10 clusters preserved gyp
1½ yards "Shimmer Lame" ribbon, size 9, from WFR Ribbon Co.
Fern pins, green florist tape, wire, florist picks

125

The traditional Christmas wreath shown in Color Fig. 11 is very easily made using a fabric-wrapped wire frame. Cut the fabric into 3-inch-wide strips, cutting on the bias. Tie one end of a fabric strip to the outside rim of the wreath frame. Wind the fabric strip around the wreath at an angle, overlapping the edges at least 1 inch. Wrap the fabric firmly, pulling the strips down firmly to the wire. Add pieces of fabric as needed by tying the ends of the fabric together, positioning the knots on the back of the frame. Tie the end of the last strip to the beginning knot. Wrapping the frame with fabric in this way makes small pockets along the top and sides of the wreath.

Collect a variety of evergreens and cut them into pieces approximately 6 to 8 inches long. Now comes the easy part. Begin to fill the "pockets" along the outside edge by pushing the ends of the evergreens between the layers of fabric. Cover the outside edge, and then the inside edge of the wreath, filling each pocket as full as possible with evergreen cuttings. Add cuttings to the center top to complete the wreath. At the end of the holidays it is very easy to remove the materials and the base is ready for adding new evergreens next season.

Begin decorating center of wreath using the gold lame ribbon, pinning the ribbon to the wreath with fern pins, twisting and turning the ribbon to make a series of raised loops around the wreath. Decorate center of wreath with 10 rose/ivy leaf clusters.

To make rose/ivy leaf cluster: Break preserved gyp into clusters approximately 6 inches long. Hold one cluster of gyp and one piece of red celosia together and tape ends together. Add one dried yellow rose at the base of the celosia, and tape the rose stem to the ends of the cluster. Add one preserved ivy leaf at the base of the rose, securing to cluster with florist tape. Wire the cluster to a florist pick and insert the cluster into the center of the wreath, covering the fern pins that are used to secure the ribbon. Around the rose clusters insert pieces of glycerine-preserved andromeda that have been sprayed gold.

At the end of the holidays, remove the rose clusters and pack away in a box for use in another wreath or design next year. The ivy leaves may turn dark brown in time, but they can be painted green. They will last indefinitely and can be used in many ways if you remove them from the rose clusters. The rose clusters may be used in other arrangements during spring or summer.

Green and Gold Mantel Decoration

Natural green roping
1½ dozen silica-dried yellow roses
1 pair Window Pockets from Taylor Crafts
Dried red celosia
Glycerine-preserved large ivy leaves
Gold-sprayed, glycerine-preserved andromeda
4 yards gold "Shimmer Lame" ribbon, size 9, from WFR Ribbon Co.
6 decorated pine cones (directions on page 132)

To make a mantel decoration like the one shown in Color Fig. 11, first measure the length of your mantel and purchase ready-made natural green roping. Or else cut and lay pieces of evergreen across the mantel (allow evergreens to dry overnight before placing on mantel to prevent sap from damaging the wood). Place the Window Pockets at each end of the mantel and arrange the roses and other materials as shown in the color figure. The window pockets contain Oasis and may be used to hold fresh materials as well as the dried flowers. Drape the gold ribbon around the ends and across the mantel, tucking it in and out of the evergreens. Add the decorated pine cones as an accent along the ribbon.

Fig. 2-32 Window pocket placement on corner of mantel. Add flowers and foliage, pushing stems into Oasis.

Topiary Centerpiece with Roses and Ivy

8-inch Styrofoam ball
24-inch wood dowel, $\frac{3}{8}$ inch diameter, sprayed gold
8-inch clay flower pot, sprayed gold
Plaster of Paris
Glue gun, florist picks, Moss Mate, wire
18 dried yellow roses
Red celosia, pearly everlasting
Glycerine-treated ivy leaves
5 yards gold "Shimmer Lame" ribbon, size 9, from WFR Ribbon Co.

The beautiful and unusual topiary centerpiece shown in Color Fig. 11 was designed by Shirley Girioni. It is basically a Styrofoam ball covered with preserved roses and ivy. When planning a centerpiece for your table, the height of the design must either be above or below the eye level of the guests. The general rule for this measurement is to place your elbow on the table and measure from the table to the tip of your finger. Your floral arrangement must be below or above this height.

The topiary is supported in a large clay flower pot filled with plaster of Paris, purchased from a hardware store. Prepare the plaster of Paris following the package directions. Cover the drainage hole in the flower pot and fill the pot with the plaster of Paris. Push the wood dowel into the center of the mixture and hold until the mixture is thick enough to support the dowel. Allow to set-up completely and get hard. Spray the dowel and flower pot with gold paint.

Push the Styrofoam ball onto the end of the dowel, adding a small amount of melted glue to the end of the dowel. Cover Styrofoam ball with green Moss Mate, cutting and fitting to fit around ball. Attach to ball using glue gun.

Wire small clusters of the dried materials to florist picks and insert into the ball, covering the ball completely. Cut 5-inch lengths of gold ribbon and wire to florist picks. Add ribbon loops to ball, pushing picks into ball. Cover top of flower pot with Moss Mate, gluing to the plaster of Paris. Add the dried flowers and ivy leaves, attaching to the Moss Mate using the glue gun. Cut the remaining ribbon into six long pieces and pin to base of topiary using fern pins.

The centerpiece may be used from year to year if protected from moisture and dust by covering with a large paper bag or soft fabric pillow case. Be careful that the dried roses are not crushed under the weight of the covering.

Fig. 2-33 Christmas tree with natural ornaments and luffa star tree top.

Christmas Ornaments

1. *Small twig wreath with bird nest (designed by Elenore Hartman):* Cut and strip honeysuckle vines of leaves and wind into a small wreath approximately 3 inches wide. Twist a small amount of Spanish moss into a small bird nest and glue to the bottom of the wreath. Glue a small bird in the nest. Decorate the top of the wreath with small dried flowers.

Fig. 2-34 Small and medium twig wreaths, decorated chipwood ornaments, corn husk doll, luffa sponge Christmas tree top.

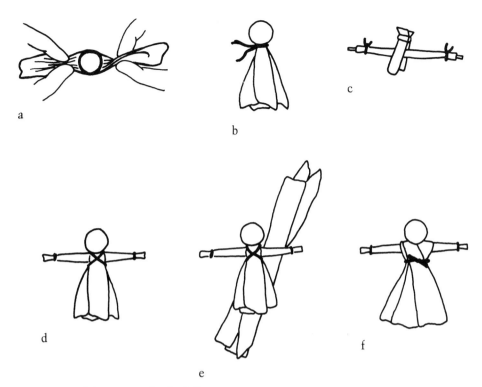

Fig. 2-35 Making a corn husk doll.

2. *Medium-sized twig wreaths (designed by Jennifer Lindgren):* Cut and strip honeysuckle vines of leaves and wind into a small wreath approximately 6 inches wide. Glue on dried flowers and glycerine leaves. Add small red cardinals or other artificial birds. Tie a 9-inch piece of narrow ribbon into a bow and glue to the top.

3. *Chipwood star and looped ornaments:* Purchase ready-made chipwood ornaments and decorate with preserved gyp and tiny dried flowers, dipping the ends of the dried materials into glue and inserting into the sides and front of the ornament.

4. *Corn husk doll:* Materials: Corn husks 6 to 8 inches long, $\frac{3}{4}$-inch diameter Styrofoam ball, white chenille stem, natural colored thread, corn silks. Remove the corn silks from a fresh ear of corn, tie the ends together and hang up to dry. When dry, braid the silks, tying the ends with matching thread. Make two braids and set aside. Soften corn husks in warm water. Select one thin, pliable corn husk and fold over Styrofoam ball, smoothing carefully to avoid splitting; tie at base of ball with thread. Cut chenille stem into a 3-inch length, wrap in a corn husk strip, tie at ends with thread. Slip arms inside corn husks at base of head and tie arms in place. Fold three to five narrow strips over each shoulder and tie at waistline, adding as many layers as needed to make a full skirt. Glue braids to top of head. Glue on a small piece of corn husk resembling a scarf or hat.

5. *Luffa star:* Purchase one large luffa from a bath shop or grow your own. Cut luffa into 1-inch wide pieces. Glue five pieces together in the shape of a star. Trim star with strawflowers glued to the center of each piece of luffa. Add pieces of dried grasses around center. Glue one teasel/lunaria flower in the center, adding a strawflower to the tip of the lunaria.

6. *Gold-painted pine cone:* Spray small pine cone with gold paint and allow to dry. Glue clusters of preserved gyp around the top and tie a gold lace ribbon into a bow around the stem. Attach a wire loop to the stem. Use on a Christmas tree or tuck into greens on a mantel.

7. *Miniature pine cone balls:* Select various small pine cones, nuts, seeds, and dried statice. Dip the ends of each cone into white glue and push the ends into a 2-inch Styrofoam ball. Complete one side and allow to dry before decorating the other side. Balls may be left in their natural colors or sprayed with gold paint. To hang, insert a wire between the cones and make a hook on the end of the wire.

8. *Small pine cone tree:* Purchase tree-shaped dyalite forms from a craft shop, or cut a small tree shape from a sheet of Styrofoam. Glue small pine cones along the sides and front of tree, allow to dry before adding cones to the back of the tree. Spray with gold paint and add a wire hook to the top of the tree.

9. *Small bird picture:* Materials: 2-inch glass disk from Houston Art and Frame Co., small bird print, lace, narrow rayon trim, ribbon, glue, cardboard, Spanish moss, dried flowers. Cut the cardboard to fit the back of the glass disk; glue small bird print to the cardboard. Form a small bird nest under bird using the moss, gluing to the picture. Add

Fig. 2-36 Pine cone ornaments.

two or three small dried flowers. Glue the lace to the edge of the card-board. Cover the picture with the glass disk, gluing the disk over the edge of the lace. Glue the narrow trim on the edge of the disk. Fold ribbon into a loop and glue to the top of the picture. Cover ends of loop with a small bow.

10. *Chenille star:* Fold two white chenille stems into small tri-angles, overlapping ends and gluing together. Glue one triangle over the other, forming the points on the star. Glue small red flowers to the star.

Fig. 2-37 Christmas ornaments: Small bird picture; chenille star; small boot covered with parsley and flowers; potpourri basket.

11. *Small boot ornament*: Purchase a dyalite Christmas boot from a craft shop or cut a small boot from Styrofoam. Cover the sides and front of boot with white glue. Sprinkle crushed dried parsley over the glue. Glue small individual flower heads over the parsley, filling the front of the boot.

12. *Christmas potpourri basket (designed by Chere Brodsky)*: Materials: Small basket; $1\frac{1}{4}$ yard pink satin ribbon, $\frac{5}{8}$ inch wide; $1\frac{1}{4}$ yard yellow satin ribbon, $\frac{1}{16}$ inch wide; $\frac{5}{8}$ yard gold-edged trim, 2 inches wide; dried roses or rose potpourri; Aleene's Designer Tacky Glue. Wrap bas-

Fig. 2-38 *Christmas ornaments: Parsley, statice, and chive ball; small bird nests on clothes pins; fluffy milkweed ball; Victorian nosegay; glass ornament trimmed with lace and flowers; decorated wicker bell.*

ket handle with pink ribbon, overlapping edges slightly. Wind yellow ribbon around handle in criss-cross design, gluing ends of ribbon on under side of handle. Fold remaining yellow ribbon into a cluster bow and glue to top of handle. Draw a small heart that will fit on the trim. Draw one heart on each end and three hearts across each side, using a washable marking pen. Crush rose buds or potpourri to a fine powder. Spread glue inside the hearts and sprinkle heavily with powdered potpourri. Shake off excess before continuing with the next heart. Glue the heart trim to top of basket, with seam at one corner.

13. *Large round dried flower ornament*: Materials: 3-inch Styrofoam ball, white glue, wire, dried parsley leaves, statice, dried chive flowers. Cover Styrofoam ball with white glue and roll in crushed dried parsley, coating the ball heavily. Allow to dry. Decorate ball with heads of dried chives and small pieces of white statice. Insert piece of wire into ball and form a hook for hanging ornament.

14. *Small bird nest (designed by Elenore Hartman):* Materials: Spanish moss, small artificial bird, clothes pins, dried flowers, glue. Form small handful of Spanish moss into a bird nest and glue to the top of a clothes pin. Decorate edges of the nest with dried flowers and place bird in center of nest.

15. *White fluffy ball:* Materials: 2-inch Styrofoam ball, glue, white flower heads of achillea, fluffy seed heads from milkweed pods, red flowers. Cover part of the ball with glue. Push a seed head from the milkweed pod into the ball and place a small white flower on the ball. Continue to fill the ball with seed heads and white flowers. Add red dried flowers around the ball, gluing the stems to the ball.

16. *Victorian nosegay:* Materials: 6-inch paper doily, 1 large head dried Queen-Anne's-Lace, assorted dried flowers, glue, gold spray paint. Spray Queen-Anne's-lace seed head with gold paint. Dip the ends of dried flowers in glue and fill the center of the seed head with the flowers. Push stem through center of paper doily and gather doily around base of seed head. Glue doily to base of seed head.

17. *Glass ornaments with lace and dried flowers:* Glue a small piece of lace around top of glass ornament. Glue small dried flowers to top.

18. *Wicker bell:* Decorate a purchased wicker ornament with ribbons, small pine cones, and preserved gyp.

Classic Colonial Fan

Classic Colonial Wood Fan frame from Taylor Crafts
Preserved magnolia leaves
Natural evergreen roping
1 pineapple, 6 large lemons, 10 large red delicious apples, 6 green
    apples
Evergreen clippings
Wire, staple gun, nails, hammer
Gold spray paint
Clear liquid floor wax
15 yards red outdoor velvet ribbon

This classic "above-the-door" decoration is shown in Color Fig. 1.
Directions for attaching fruit to fan are included with the ready-to-use

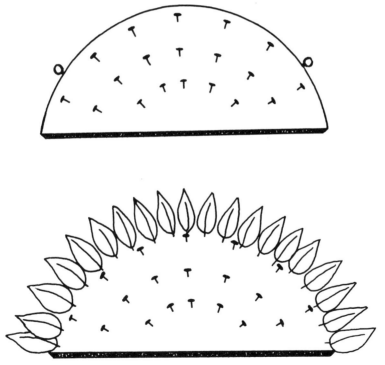

Fig. 2-39 Placement of nails and magnolia leaves on Colonial fan.

wood frame. The frame is a green-stained wooden form 38 inches by 9 inches and comes with nails and rings for easy hanging above a door. Attach nails on wood frame in pre-marked spots, nailing them at an upward angle to support the fruit. Attach metal rings to the pre-marked spots on outer edge of fan. Position fan above door and mark the placement of long heavy nails from which to hang the fan. The rings will be slipped over these nails for hanging the fan.

The fan is heavy when covered with the fruit and you may wish to attach a strip of wood to the top of your door frame as a base to support the fan. Paint the wood strip to match the color of your house, staple pieces of evergreen to the front edge.

Spray the green magnolia leaves with gold paint and staple to the front of the fan. Measure around the door frame and purchase the amount of evergreen roping needed for your door. Nail one heavy nail at each corner of the door and one in the center of the door frame. Hang the roping across the top of the door, ends extending down as far as needed on the sides. Wire the roping to these nails and to nails placed at each of the bottom ends.

Position the pineapple on the center of the fan, placing wire around the top of the pineapple, and running the wire through the wood in the pre-drilled holes. Twist the wire tightly on the back of the frame.

I recommend that the fan be put in place above the door at this time because the fan is so heavy when finished that one person cannot position it easily. Slip the rings over the nails and check to be sure the fan is securely placed on the door frame. I nailed each end of the fan into the door frame for extra support.

Dip apples into clear floor wax and allow to dry before using. Push apples and lemons onto the nails, tipping the fruit at an angle to prevent them from sliding off. Fill in open spaces around fruit and at the top and bottom of the fan using small cuttings of evergreens. Cut ribbon into 3 yard lengths and tie into large bows. Wire bows to top of door and posts as shown.

Fig. 2-40 Apple tree framed in pine cones and natural greens for the front door.

Apple Tree for Door

Wooden tree form from Taylor Crafts
30 to 35 large Norway spruce or other pine cones
3 large red delicious apples, 6 green apples, 1 grapefruit
Clear liquid floor wax, glue gun

The green stained wooden tree form comes with wire that should be formed into a loop and attached to back of the tree with a nail. Attach nails to the front of the tree on the pre-marked spots, placing at an upward angle to support the fruit.

Select pine cones as near the same size as possible, and glue around the outside edge of the tree as pictured in Fig. 2-41. Glue the pine cones to each other at the spots where they touch for extra security. Spray the pine cones with clear plastic lacquer to add extra shine. Dip the apples into the clear plastic floor wax and allow to dry on a sheet of wax paper. Position the apples on the tree as pictured in Fig. 2-40. Fill in openings around fruit with small evergreen cuttings, tucking behind the fruit.

Tie 3 yards of red outdoor ribbon into a large bow and wire to the bottom of the tree. Hang the tree on a nail in the center of the door.

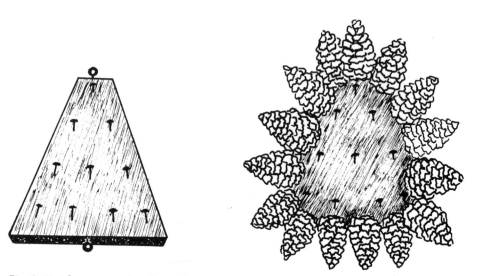

Fig. 2-41 Placement of nails and pine cones on the apple tree.

Colonial Fruit Cone

12-inch wooden cone from Taylor Crafts
8 large lemons, 10 to 12 limes
10 to 12 pine cones
12 large gold yarrow
Natural evergreen clippings
Gold spray paint
Glue gun

Spray pine cones with gold spray paint and set aside. Hammer the nails into the wooden cone in the pre-marked spots. Place the nails at an upward angle to support the lemons and limes. Place one large lemon on the top of the cone (see Color Fig. 11). Add lemons and limes to the sides of the cone. Glue pine cones in between the fruit. Fill in any open spaces with small cuttings of evergreens to complete the cone. The fruit and pine cones will support the evergreens. Add pieces of gold yarrow, slipping the stems behind the pine cones or fruit.

The cone may be displayed in the center of the growing ivy wreath

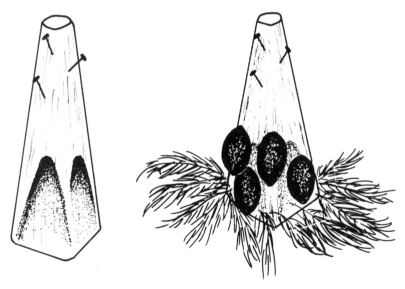

Fig. 2-42 Making a Colonial fruit cone.

as pictured or on a table as a centerpiece, adding pieces of evergreens and other pieces of fruit to fill out the centerpiece. The fruit should last through the holidays if placed in a cool spot in the house. Remove fruit and evergreens, leaving the pine cones attached for use during the next holiday season. Save the gold yarrow also for next year.

A traditional Colonial decoration can be made using the same cone shape by adding a large pineapple to the top and filling in the sides of the cone with large red apples. Dip the apples into clear floor wax to help preserve their freshness, and allow to dry before placing on the cone. Fill in the open spaces with cuttings of evergreens.

Artemesia Wreath with White Lights

14-inch double box wire wreath
1 string white Italian Christmas lights
Artemesia, pearly everlasting, blue salvia, blue heather, blue and white statice
Preserved gyp from Lamrite's
3 yards "Super Beau Vel" ribbon, size 9, color 807 from WFR Ribbon Co.
Florist picks, white florist tape
Wire, glue or glue gun

An artemesia wreath laced with tiny white lights makes a very special holiday decoration, as seen in color Fig. 6. Remove the flower heads from each stem of artemesia, leaving a 3-inch length of stem, and set aside. Hold the heavy artemesia stems together and attach to the wire wreath with florist wire. Overlap the ends as needed, filling the base with at least a 1-inch thickness of artemesia. The direction of placement of the artemesia isn't important as it will be covered with the other decorative materials. Use fresh artemesia if possible because the stems are pliable and easier to shape. The wreath can be made in the fall and saved for Christmas display.

Cover the green wires on the string of Christmas lights with white florist tape. Attach the lights to the artemesia base, placing the plug end at the bottom of the wreath. Use fern pins to hold each small light

142

and the wires in place. Scatter the lights around the wreath on the front and sides, and plug in the lights to check the placement before decorating with other materials.

Beginning at the top of the wreath, add the artemesia flower heads, dipping the ends into glue or using the glue gun and inserting the stems into the artemesia base. Decorate each side of the wreath with the flower heads facing toward the center bottom of the wreath. Do not cover and hide the white lights, but move the flower heads so that each light is supported in a cluster of flowers.

Wire small clusters of pearly everlasting to florist picks and decorate the center of the wreath all the way around. Hold together four or five pieces of blue salvia and trim to a length of about 6 inches. Place the blue salvia around the inside and outside of the pearly everlasting, pushing the stems deep into the base. Cut 6-inch pieces of blue heather and scatter around the wreath as needed to add color. Heather is very fragile when dry and must be handled carefully. Purchased heather may be preserved in glycerine, which makes it easier to handle and transfer to other arrangements without shattering. Heather should be preserved when the flowers are fresh and have just opened on the stems.

Tie the blue ribbon into a bow and wire to the top of the wreath. Attach a piece of wire on the back to make a loop for hanging the wreath.

Blue and White Sideboard Decor

The antique sideboard in Color Fig. 6 was made by my great-grandfather from black walnut wood that he cut and prepared. He made all the furniture for his family's home in Iowa in the early 1800s. Cobalt blue compote dishes are used as containers for the dried arrangements. A piece of Oasis was added to the compote, held in place with florist clay. The curved material is pieces of blue spruce, trimmed as needed to expose the natural curves in the branches. Select pieces of artemesia that have curved flower heads and repeat the curved line of the blue spruce. Fill in the arrangement with stems of blue salvia, blue heather, and white pearly everlasting, wiring the pearly everlasting to floral picks or a natural stem to lengthen the flower stems.

Complete the arrangement by placing a blue candle in a small glass dish, add clusters of blue glass grapes and place on a crocheted doily.

The colors used for the sideboard decor and wreath were chosen to coordinate with the colors in my dining and living room. Choose materials and colors that fit the color scheme in your dining room, coloring the dried materials if necessary to get the colors you need.

Fig. 2-43 Table centerpiece using natural greens, blue and white dried materials, and blue glass grapes. See Color Fig. 6.

Dining Table Centerpiece

9-by-12-inch piece Styrofoam
3 blue candles, 14 inches high
2 yards ribbon cut into 9-inch pieces
Blue salvia, heather, preserved gyp, artemesia, blue spruce
Floral picks, wire

    Refer to Fig. 2-44 and cut Styrofoam into pieces as indicated. Glue the pieces together to make a wedding cake shape. Insert the candles into sides and top of the Styrofoam as shown, pushing the candles in until they are secure. Cut various lengths of blue spruce and other natural greens and push the ends into the Styrofoam, covering the base completely.

    Decorate the centerpiece with clusters of dried flowers, wiring the clusters to floral picks and inserting the picks between the branches of evergreens. Wire the loops of ribbon to a florist pick and add to the centerpiece. Decorate with clusters of blue glass grapes.

    At the end of the holidays, remove the dried flowers from the centerpiece and the sideboard arrangements and pack away in a box for use next year. Throw away the evergreens. Save the Styrofoam base for use in another arrangement.

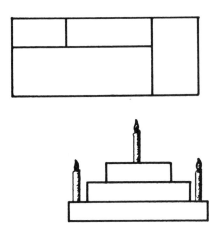

Fig. 2-44 How to cut Styrofoam and place candles for the centerpiece.

Red and White Heart Wreath

17-inch straw heart covered with Spanish moss, from Lamrite's
1 bunch red happy flowers, 4 oz. preserved gyp from Lamrite's
1 large branch lunaria (money plant)
4 to 5 clusters achillea
3 small red cardinals
2 yards red picot double-wired ribbon, size 40, and 3 yards red "Super
    Beau Vel" ribbon, size 9, from WFR Ribbon Co.
Fern pins, glue, wire, red spray paint

Gather the double-wired ribbon to fit the back of the heart wreath by pinching the ribbon together into small tucks along one of the wired edges. Attach the gathered ribbon to the wreath using fern pins placed in the small holes along the edge of the ribbon. Twist a length of wire into a loop and attach to the back of the heart with a fern pin.

Spray the achillea with the red spray paint. To decorate the heart, break the preserved gyp, lunaria, and red achillea into small clusters about 4 to 5 inches. Wire small bunches of red happy flowers to a florist pick. Cover the front of the heart with the red and white dried materials as shown in Color Fig. 16. Dip the stems of the lunaria, gyp, and achillea into glue and insert into the moss, pushing the stems through the moss and into the straw base. Add the red cardinals, inserting the wires into the base. Tie the narrow red ribbon into a large bow and wire to the top of the wreath.

Suspend the heart wreath from a length of ribbon, wiring the ribbon to a small nail in the center of the door. Cover the nail with a small bow. The wreath may be used outdoors if on a porch partially protected from the weather.

Red and White Winter Bouquets

White wicker floral baskets
Sumac, teasel, plumed celosia
Lunaria, artemesia
Baby's breath, phragmites, Queen-Anne's-Lace

6 to 8 contrived teasel flowers
Large Styrofoam egg
4½ yards red picot double-wired ribbon, size 40 from WFR Ribbon Co.
White florist tape
White and red spray paint

As seen in Color Fig. 16, a beautiful red and white winter bouquet can be made from dried weeds collected late in the winter. This type of bouquet would be very attractive as a winter wedding decoration, especially for Valentine's Day.

Spray the dried weeds and baby's breath with the white spray paint, allowing to dry before arranging. Remove the stickers from the teasel stems and spray the heads with red paint. Spray the sumac berry clusters and heads of the plumed celosia with red paint.

Refer to instructions in Part One for making contrived flowers and make lunaria-teasel flowers.

When all materials are prepared and ready to use, insert the large Styrofoam egg into the opening of the floral basket with the narrow end down. If an egg shape is not available, trim a block of Styrofoam to fit the narrow opening in the basket. Begin placing the white phragmites to the back of the basket using the largest and tallest heads, pushing the stems deep into the Styrofoam. Add long stems of lunaria, artemesia, Queen-Anne's-lace, and the red painted materials. Add false stems if necessary with the florist tape. Fill basket with the red and white materials, placing the teasel flowers to the front of the design. Tie the red ribbon into a large bow and wire to front of basket.

The arrangements are suitable for outdoor decoration if the porch is partially protected from wind and rain.

To decorate a doorway as shown in the color photograph, measure around the door frame and purchase natural green roping. Place a large nail at each corner of the door frame and wire the roping to the nail for support. Purchase 5 yards of outdoor ribbon for each large bow. Measure around the glass insert on the door and purchase ribbon double that measurement. Gather the double-wired ribbon by pinching one edge of the ribbon into small tucks. The wire in the ribbon will hold the gathers in place. Attach the ribbon to the glass or wood molding using double-face tape. Small push pins or finishing nails may be used to secure the ribbon at the corners.

Sources of Supplies

Craft Supplies

Activa Products, Inc.
PO Box 1296
Marshall, TX 75670
(Silica gel and glycerine)

Artis, Inc.
Box 407
Solvang, CA 93463
(Aleene's Designer Tacky Glue,
  Right-On)

Bentwood, Inc.
PO Box 1676
Thomasville, GA 31792
(Wedge-wood cheese box)

Craft Source
Temple City, CA 91790
(Wyndo-Cards)

Hartman Designs
153 Highmeadow Road
Guilford, CT 06437
(Florals for weddings and
  special occasions)

Houston Art and Frame
PO Box 27164
Houston, TX 77027
(Glass discs)

K.I.T.I., Inc.
PO Box 368
Woodstock, IL 60098
(Wire kissing ball,
  wire star, wire heart)

Lamrite's
565 Broadway CB
Bedford, OH 44146
(Dried flowers and floral products;
  $2.00 for catalogue)

Mountain Farms, Inc.
108 Candlewood
New Fairfield, CT 06812
(Pine cone catalogue)

MPR Associates, Inc.
PO Box 7342
High Point, NC 27264
(Nylon sleeve for potpourri kissing ball)

Sudberry House
Box 895
Old Lyme, CT 06371
(Wood products for framing
  dried flower projects)

Taylor Crafts
445 Remington Ave.
Thomasville, GA 31792
(Colonial apple cone, Apple tree,
  Classic Colonial Fan, Window
  pockets)

Topiary, Inc.
41 Berring
Tampa, FL 33606
(Topiary supplies and products)

WFR Ribbon Corp.
115 W. 18 Street
New York, NY 10011

Weeds and Wilds
Shirley Girioni
108 Highwood Dr.
Guilford, CT 06437
(Floral decorations for all occasions)

Seed and Plant Catalogues

Burpee Gardens
300 Park Ave.
Warminster, PA 18991

Park Seed
Greenwood, SC 29647

Spring Hill
PO Box 1758
Peoria, IL 61656

Wayside Gardens
Hodges, SC 29695

White Flower Farm
Litchfield, CT 06759-0050

Dried Flowers and Herbs

Cramer's Posie Patch
Box 429, RD 2
Columbia, PA 17512

Heartscents
PO Box 1674
Hilo, Hawaii 96721-1674

Herbitage Farm
RFD 2, Old Homestead Highway
Richmond, NH 03470

The Herb Patch
Middletown Springs, VT 05757

Hidden Hollow Herbiary
Elaine Van Dien N88
W18407 Duke St.
Menomonee Falls, WI 53051

Lamrite's
565 Broadway CB
Bedford, OH 44146

Le Jardin du Gormet
West Danville, VT 05873

Pennyroyal Place
72 E. Main St.
Westborough, MA 01581

Potpourri (Quarterly Newsletter from
Herbal Acres)
Pine Row Publications
Box 428
Washington Crossing, PA 18977

The Sandymush Herb Nursery
RT 2 Surrett Cove Road
Leichester, NC 28748

Sunkempt
PO Box 231
Yorkville, NY 13495